PRAISE FOR *GO MULTISPORT*

"If it feels like an adventure to you, then it is an adventure! Multisport gives you the freedom to interpret adventure in the way that works for you."

—**Alastair Humphreys**, National Geographic
Adventurer of the Year

"Jennifer has done an incredible job providing us all with a clear and concise picture of how important and powerful adventure can be in all of our lives. A book that I'll be sharing with my daughters as well, as they embark on their own paths of adventure!"

—**Ray Zahab**, Arctic world record holder &
author of *Running for My Life*

"*Go Multisport* offers fun, inspirational advice for adding spice to our exercise, training, adventures, and life. We have more than one set of muscles and using them all while outdoors makes us feel better, healthier, more centered, and complete. Jennifer McConachie shows us how."

—**Roman Dial**, author of *Packrafting*! and
national bestseller *The Adventurer's Son*

GO
MULTISPORT

ADD FUN, CHALLENGE

& EXPLORATION

TO YOUR WORLD

Jennifer Strong McConachie

Hatherleigh Press is committed to preserving and protecting
the natural resources of the earth. Environmentally
responsible and sustainable practices are embraced
within the company's mission statement.

Visit us at www.hatherleighpress.com.

GO MULTISPORT

Text Copyright © 2023 Jennifer Strong McConachie

Library of Congress Cataloging-in-Publication Data is available.

ISBN: 978-1-57826-992-1

Printed in the United States

10 9 8 7 6 5 4 3 2 1

CONTENTS

MULTISPORT

A New Adventure

The island is sinking like Atlantis into the ocean. I, however, am far from the ocean. I am on a deserted island, in the middle of a lake, in the middle of Kansas, in the middle of the United States.

I swam here.

After I hike across this submerged, watery bog, I am going to swim back to land, despite the thunderstorm and pelting rain hitting my wet skin. But first, I must tow a kayak and hike across a soaking swampland as I navigate this island covered in 400-year-old timbers. There are so many fallen trees, it is like wading through sticks. How did I come to this storming, wild place? I ran, through a hardwood forest while the skies roared above me. Next, I will bike, kayak, and stand up paddleboard back to civilization, after more open-water swimming.

I want to invite you to come with me on this multi-sport journey.

With multisport, you can participate in life as you walk the edge and blaze your own trail. You can feel the bliss of accomplishment that no one can take away. Enjoy the harmony of self-propulsion. Free yourself from constraints as you take on the role of inventor and connector. Adopt the multisport lifestyle and join the multisport movement with me.

Let's go multisport.

A Bit of Background

I am a lifelong outdoor runner, wild swimmer, mountaineer, paddler, triathlete, adventure racer, and multisport athlete. I have traveled the globe, racing in ultramarathons, climbing Seven Summits, and swimming oceans, always in search of the next level of endurance athletics.

Multisport is now *the* movement in endurance sport.

The multisport concept is both a global and local way of being a diverse athlete—a way of participating in multiple human-powered sports in one outing. Previous sports have trended toward linear definitions. If you run fast, you are a runner. If you run a long way, you are an ultrarunner. But what if you could run, climb, swim, bike, ski, snowshoe, row, skate, sail, raft, and more—all at once? This is what lifelong, pioneering athletes are discovering. Multisport is where the best, most fit, and all-around endurance athletes are finding a home in sport. This isn't the downtown 5ks, it isn't sprint triathlons—it is adventure racing, but in a new way that can fit anyone's time, budget, destination and distance. Multisport is the next "it" sport.

Are you ready to try it?

When you do, you will open a world of possibility and promise.

My first book, *Go Far: How Endurance Sports Help You Win At Life*, was a culmination of what I experienced in 30 years of competing in endurance sports and living an adventurous life as an ordinary person with an extraordinary approach to fitness, life and training.

I heard so much positive feedback from that first book, with readers asking for more stories, more ways to go out and find adventure. Multisport is the best way I have found to do that. Whether you are an athlete, a half marathoner, a marathoner, a triathlete, a parent, or a fitness newbie who wants to discover more; if you want more than your typical races, lengths, and disciplines, multisport is your next step. Multisport is your *answer*. And I want to help you reach this next degree in sport by combining events to create your own version of *Go Multisport*.

The possibilities that come with multisport and the creative aspect of breaking free of the usual, mundane, boring run, swim, bike training are endless and invigorating. Multisport gives you the opportunity to change your world in a radical way. You can start small with what you are already doing and with what you already have around you. With the *Go Multisport* mentality, you can go big too, tackling multi-hour, multi-day, and even multi-continent events.

My multisport lifestyle was the result of creating an added challenge to whatever training I was doing during a particular time or on a given day. It was also a way to put fun into that day's workout, as well as offering a way of exploring a new path or new route, connecting the world around me. When you add this multidisciplinary approach to fitness, you gain the benefits of a challenge to your traditional workout, make more fun, and go new places.

Go Multisport gives you the tools, the skill, and the know-how to create your own event. It allows you to dream, plan, think, and execute adventures that are uniquely yours. Sure, you could do a pre-existing race where all you must do is show up. But when you are striving to achieve and complete something that has not been done before, when you have an idea that is innovative, groundbreaking, and out there, multisport gives you a path to execute that idea. Multisport is planning, plotting, discovering, pushing. It is doing something that didn't exist in your way or in your combination before.

How you go about creating your adventure is important. Multisport gives you a roadmap and a set of guidelines on how to build your own versions of adventure racing and its elements. After all the sports, I am at heart, an adventure seeker. Multisport gives you adventure without the race or added logistics imposed by outside forces. It puts the power back in your hands and gives you an opportunity to execute it as close as your backyard with more sports and more fun taking you farther than ever before.

My passion is for human-powered endurance adventures that allow us to live our lives to the fullest outdoors. This self-propulsion focus personalizes the journey and places emphasis on the nature of the journey. Multisport allows us to combine self-propelled transport elements to create what we need when we need it. This revolutionary concept will help you set fast times and new records inward and out.

Multisport is the ultimate act of reinvention. Wherever you are in your sporting life, you can find a multisport combination that fits, grows, and adapts with you. Multisport was always there for me in my life, like when I needed a change, when I was injured from one activity, when life demanded adaptability, and when I craved the roar of something new.

By combining all my endurance sports, skills, and base training into new adventures, I could have and create right at home, however near or far time and circumstance allowed for, multisport was a life-enriching and life-giving hobby I could add as an individual athlete, a team player, a wife, a daughter, a Siberian husky parent, and a new mom.

Multisport will expand your world. It will broaden your thinking and it will extend your fitness base. Add fun, challenge, and exploration to your future with *Go Multisport!*

1 | What is Multisport?

Simply put, multisport is the combination of two or more sports, which allows for the creation of unique versions of sports focused on what interests *you*.

Traditionally, multisport has meant triathlons—a combination event that includes the three sports of swimming, biking and running. (In an off-road triathlon, these sports are the more rugged versions of open water swimming, mountain biking and trail running.)

Nowadays, adventure racing provides another type of traditional multisport or sporting combination. Adventure racing expands the three disciplines of triathlon and their off-road versions to include paddling sports like kayaking, canoeing, and rafting, among others. Trekking portions, obstacle challenges, and ropes and climbing courses are also key components of an adventure race, as are the navigation and orienteering skills that each team must master to complete the race.

Triathlons follow the same pattern of sport each time: swim, bike, run. The distances can vary; however, the three core sports and order stay the same.

Each adventure race, on the other hand, features routes, distances, and sports predetermined by the race director.

Oftentimes, these are influenced by the specific geographic features of the location of the event.

The magic of multisport is that unlike triathlon and adventure racing where there is a set order and the sports are chosen by someone else, with multisport *you* get to choose what sports you do, use and combine. All you must do is combine two or more human-powered sports. By choosing your own self-propelled sports, you create the multisport event that is exactly right for you.

Whenever you combine sports completed by your own propulsion, you are creating a multisport. But most importantly, you are creating a multifaceted approach to fitness.

Multisport's focus on more than one sport allows you to grow as a person as you learn new sports and take on new skills. Participating in multisport gives you the opportunity to focus on personal development from a variety of angles, as you train in multiple sports, disciplines, and varieties of fitness that fulfill a full range of developmental goals.

In learning to see everyday sport activities in new ways, we also learn to look at our world and its opportunities from fresh perspectives. Multisport encourages us to travel in the area around us right where we are. By creating homegrown adventures that you can have by going out your door, or not too far from it, multisport inspires us to create mini expeditions from home and create our own joy by doing so. As you learn the multisport mindset, you can take on adventures when you travel, or they can inspire your travel as well.

This focus on exploration via multisport encourages us to seek out the new. When you explore new ways of getting places externally, you also travel to new places internally, which is part of the added challenge aspect that multisport brings.

Traditional Multisport

When looking at the history and tradition of multisport, we can start with triathlon, duathlon, biathlon, aquathon, pentathlon, heptathlon, and decathlon sport combinations. (Adventure racing can also fall under this category, though it is a relative newcomer to the scene.) So before we start getting into the nitty-gritty of creating our own multisport experiences, let's take a look at each of these traditional offerings, including some stories from my own experiences with them, and then build into the modern multisport space . . . and how it is revolutionizing everything that has come before.

Triathlon

Perhaps the most familiar multisport is **triathlon**. Triathlon's modern beginnings start in 1970s California with the birth of the swim/bike/run combination. In triathlon, athletes compete to not only test their endurance in one sport, but in three distinct areas. As a triathlete, time must be dedicated to training in each segment. Distance and speed must be accounted for in this training, with times ranging from short sprints to Olympic and Ironman distances to ultra-extreme lengths. Triathlon sets the base for multisport today. Not only must multisport athletes train for one sport, but they must also prepare their bodies for the specific demands each arena brings.

Depending on the event, swim training can take place in a pool or open water. Bike training can be accomplished on a variety of bike types and styles, including road racing bikes, triathlon bikes that maximize aerodynamics, and mountain bikes in off-road versions. Run training involves endurance and fast interval training, and even the vagaries of trail hills and climbs to attune to the individual event demands.

I was drawn to the specialization in more than one zone, and as my triathlon experience grew, so did the different race lengths, distances, and off-road options.

The combination of triathlon's three events continued to grow in popularity and was at one of its peaks when I first started competing in the 1990s.

I spent my childhood racing triathlons around the Midwest. Every summer, I traveled the country competing in the Ironkids triathlon series. My hair was always in braids to keep it contained while swimming, biking, and running, and then paddling, and other sports in later years. I was a strong competitor mentally and physically from those early races. I gained confidence and endurance for life, in addition to family friends.

I trained around my neighborhood parkland with my dad, looping around our family rivers on bikes and runs. My swim training came from daily club swim team workouts. Each spring, I also prepared for the opening weekend race that kicked off the series in my hometown by practicing my relished transitions. I exercised test runs from swimming to biking and biking to running in our living room by laying out all my gear, piece by piece on an old beach towel, trimmed to the perfect size to fit next to my bike below my dedicated tri bag. I would run from my bedroom in my racing swimsuit practicing at full speed the long run from the indoor pool to the outdoor transition area in the grassy lawn.

I would then go through each step of taking off my swim cap and goggles while still running, and throwing on my required racing shirt with pinned-on bib number, cropped to be as light as possible, in addition to being '90s stylish. I coiled the race shirt up to its smallest size with only the bib number and safety pins balancing on the towel so that I could bend down and throw it on via the arm holes as fast as I could, while also sliding on my lightweight racing shoes with the laces cut, ends burned, and shoelace lock toggles attached to avoid the cumbersome task of tying my shoes mid-transition.

After donning my bike helmet, I met the minimum gear requirements of shoes, shirt with bib number, and safety helmet. I would execute an imaginary un-rack of my bike and sprint outside to practice hopping on, with one leg swung over mid-stride, and take off down the driveway to mimic a real-life race. The swim to bike transition was the most technical and I was a speed demon. I loved being fast and light, my transition art practiced down to a science.

The next leg of bike to run transition was even quicker, as all I had to do was hop off my bike mid-pedal, rack it, throw off my helmet, grab my Oakley sunglasses (all the podium finishers wore Oakley M-frames) and sprint out of the gate at a full-tilt run toward the finish arch ahead.

A triathlon can easily be won or lost in these transitions. My speed at these, through practice and nightly step-by-step visualizations, proved itself through the years on almost every adventure race, mountain climb and multisport adventure. Learning how to go from one sport to another and assemble my gear properly was an early multisport skill learned from triathlons, one I value both for its general usefulness and its ability to segue into other sporting areas.

After training and transition practices, I would show up to the college campus on race day and carefully assemble my gear in the transition areas before heading to the gym by the pool to anxiously await my age group heat. Our racing numbers always started with our age. This allowed you to know who you were racing against while on the course. You wanted to win your age group. We wore these number badges of permanent marker inked up and down our arms and legs with pride for days before they faded away. They showed the world that we were more than just kids. We were triathletes.

Another badge of honor was the coveted watch tan. Watches were not allowed during the race. If you showed up in the gym, lined up in your age group heat with the rolled up wrestling mats sporting a watch tan, you were a true competitor. The watch tan showed that you had trained outside in the sun enough to earn a tan. I still show off my watch tan today as a sign that I have been out and taken hold of the training, the adventure and life outside.

I raced my guts out during those triathlon days. I loved the challenge of training for and competing in three sports combined into one. Each leg offered a new way to push and race.

As soon as I was tired of one event, a new one entered. I collected medals and lined our garage, full of cross training equipment and an indoor bike trainer, with racing numbers from events up and down the country. After each event, my dad and I would staple the Tyvek, paper, and cardboard race numbers on the old 1920s wooden slats in our all-weather gym area. This rainbowed collection of numbers, colors, and sizes motivated me during training, inspired me to take on more, and cemented my role early in life as a multisport athlete. I learned race strategy and training tips from my dad, as my mom devoted every Mother's Day and summer weekend to triathlon and racing.

After I aged out of Ironkids, I delved into more school and club events, continuing to run and swim competitively, among other sports, and bike for adventure.

After middle and high school sports, I went to college for Division I rowing. During the winter season of my fist college crew year, one weekend the coaches organized an all-team indoor triathlon of pool swimming, erging—as the indoor row-ers were called—and running around the old-school track arena.

The pool swim portion was simple. I swam competitively as an age grouper so I always felt comfortable in the pool. Coupled with my childhood triathlon racing experience, the pool swim portion of this triathlon was easy. We occasionally included pool workouts as part of rowing training, and I always excelled on those days. I was happy in the water. Erging is short for ergometer, devices used to measure the amount of work done by a group of muscles. On the erg, the harder you go, the more resistance you get.

I never liked the erg; I preferred to be outside, racing in a scull boat and training on the water in the wild elements of the outdoors. I did feel a deep connection to Ahearn Field House on the Kansas State University campus where the indoor tri took place. The sweat of generations of past K-State athletes still hung in the air. I loved roaming about the bowels of this building and its connecting natatorium. When I was near Ahearn, I was home. Sprinting around the track in this venerable old field house recalled my days as a child track athlete. I moved fast and free on the run, even if indoors, as I was away from the measuring, counting, tethering erg.

The rowing triathlon was easier for me than any rowing practice or regatta, I soon learned. I was happy swimming, running, and winning. This event rekindled my love for the original multisport of triathlon.

This hybrid triathlon also led me to go back to something that I was suited to: Endurance and the combination of three sports rooted in endurance combined into one.

This event was a pivotal moment in my life. It was the tipping point that allowed me to realize I wanted to return to triathlon.

In triathlon, I learned that the swim is about instinct. I loved the water and I loved to swim, but an open-water triathlon swim is different. First, you are in the middle of a lake. There are no lane lines and no flags to guide you. You only have the buoys in the far distance. Then, you are missing the use of several senses. You can't feel because you are wearing a wetsuit. You can't see because the lake water is silty brown, you are swimming into the sun, and the splash of the other swimmers and fog on your goggles makes everything white. You can't breathe because you are underwater, and when you tilt your head for air, the waves jolt into your mouth. On top of this, it is a battle. Hundreds of swimmers are fighting for the buoy line. You swim over and under feet, arms and legs. The swim is not about swimming; it is about survival. It is about putting your head down and going. It is about getting back to land as fast as you possibly can.

In triathlon, the bike is about your engine. How much cardio and how much leg power do you have? And how long can you sit in the saddle and work it?

Finally, a triathlon run is about guts. Short or long, I have never raced a triathlon that is not about guts once the run starts. Your energy is spent and the only way to make it through is to gut it out.

My triathlon swim experiences were fast and quick, and I would emerge as race leader. We always felt that the swimming portion of triathlon events could be longer to better mirror the bike and run distances required. I slogged through the bike portions on hills and routes and gave everything else that was left on my final runs. From lake to pool, from trail to road, I raced as a young college student in between life, work, teaching group fitness classes, and studying.

Having these base sport experiences in triathlon informed my multisport creation later in life so that instead of focusing on survival, power, and guts only, I could also focus on challenging myself in a more fun, energizing way that multisport brings, while continuing to explore new areas. Keeping what I enjoyed about triathlon helped me build and create my multisport.

Duathlon

A **duathlon** combines the two sports of biking and running. A duathlon can be a bike/run or a bike/run/bike, with the three legs mirroring the three of triathlon, but only including two sports. Distances and terrains in duathlon vary depending on the type and style of the racing event.

During my triathlon days, I would often compete in duathlons when the weather turned stormy or unsafe for outdoor swimming. For example, several times the swim portions of a triathlon event were cancelled due to weather conditions, and I competed in a makeshift bike/run or bike/run/bike duathlon race. Typically, a duathlon combines biking and running, however, with multisport concepts, you can create your own style of multisport duathlon by combining two human-powered endurance events together into one at one go. They could be biking and running, or any other two that you dream up. In multisport, a duathlon could even include a bike/run rotational event that I will profile in the coming pages. Multisport lets us crush the boundaries of traditional duathlon parameters.

Biathlon

The traditional **biathlon** is a winter sport that combines cross country skiing and rifle shooting. Competitors follow a cross country ski route, stopping at shooting ranges along the way. Shots are taken either standing up, lying down, or a combination of both. Shots missed can result in time added to your finish time. Biathlon has roots in Scandinavia and was born out of military training that took place in those hardy, cold locales.

On a summer home from college, I competed in a summer-style biathlon, where I ran one mile, shot several blank rounds at a target, ran one mile, shot, and then ran a final mile for three miles of running total with two rounds of lying down target shooting. My dad rode his bike to the race site, about 20 miles away, and then competed in the event, and biked home add even more to the multisporting day's range.

I was amazed how hard it was to focus on hitting a target after sprinting, lying down in the grass, sweat dripping into my eyes and down my skin, with my breath gasping, as I focused my aim on the target. I think I missed every shot but ran fast enough in between to win my age group, even with time added for those missed shots.

Cross country skiing, running, and biking can be incorporated into your own biathlon multisport event with shooting targets. Archery could be rotated in for the shooting portions as another or additional multisport component. A biathlon with a paddle, archery target range, paddle, archery target would be another creative multisport take on the traditional biathlon, building boating and the classic survival skill of archery into your multisport.

Aquathon

An **aquathon** is a swimming and running race with transitions between the two. In an aquathon you might run three miles, have a transition, swim a mile, have a transition, and then run another three miles.

An aquathon is similar to a duathlon in that it includes two sports.

An evolution of the sport of aquathon is the **swimrun**. In the new swimrun multisport I competed in, there were no transitions between the two. I alternated running and swimming, going from water to trail in one fluid movement, often for ultramarathon-like distances and times, through and across chains of islands in cold-water climates.

Aquathons were more like triathlons with shorter distances, more contained, monitored courses, and transitions. Swimruns were more thrilling due to taking place in cold open water, pathless running that required more individual navigation, hardened conditions, and for much longer distances.

Aquathon and the evolved swimrun concepts are huge components of my multisport events today, as they combine two of my favorite sports, swimming and running, and the idea of going without a transition for one long, continuous multisport day or days.

Pentathlon

Modern **pentathlon** combines five different sports: fencing, swimming, equestrian, shooting, and cross country running. It is inspired by the event held at the ancient Olympics patterned on the skills needed by an ideal Greek solider at the time.

Heptathlon & Decathlon

Similar to pentathlon, a **heptathlon** is made up of seven track and field events, whereas a **decathlon** combines 10 track and field events. Each of these takes the Greek prefix number and suffix of -athlons, which is Greek for competition.

The multisports of today draw elements from each of these traditional combinations as well as from adventure racing to create their own version of sport combos that unite formality, hazard and experience. With that said, let's discuss adventure racing a little bit—what it is, what it *isn't*, and what modern multisport takes from it to create something brand new.

How Multisport Differs From Adventure Racing

Adventure racing takes the essence behind all of these types of races and adds in that secret ingredient: the unknown factor. In traditional -athlon racing, things are measured, succinct and ruled. Adventure racing is about making your own route and way to reach your control point. What sets multisport apart from triathlon and adventure racing is that you design the route.

In adventure racing, control points, or checkpoints are used to keep you on track. How you navigate to each one is often up to your individual team, but you move from each segment, sport, and section as determined by the event organizer.

In multisport, you determine where you want to go, what route you will take, what you want to encounter and incorporate along the way, and what sports you will use to do so, and in what order you want to do them. If you want to have checkpoints, or check-in points for safety, you can, but they are not required.

Adventure racing combines trail running, mountain biking, kayaking, canoeing, trekking, orienteering, lake and river swim crossings, rappelling, navigation, and obstacle challenges, all linked together in a race. Depending on the location, sports relating to that area can also be mixed into adventure racing, such as rafts, specialized regional boats, inline skates, or canyoneering.

One of my favorite aspects of adventure racing that I use when building multisports is using the area and climate to influence the way I make and guide my event. I liked the variables and unknowns adventure racing offered. It was more rugged than traditional triathloning. Triathlons were structured and supported. Adventure racing took place in wilderness areas with minimal outside support. Teams were often in charge of their own food and hydration needs for an event. Adventure racing also called for strategy, as teams mapped their own courses and charted routes to the checkpoints. Success demanded more wit and pluck.

Like triathlon, multisport can take place in the city, on a road, trail, or in a daily urban route. You can stash fuel along the way or with family and friends for a supported event. Like adventure racing, multisport can take place near lakeshores, grasslands, refuges, scenic waterways and wild lands. You can haul your own water and fuel to make it self-supported or choose to have assistance along the way.

In multisport, the strategy often comes into play before an event, where you research and make your routes and plans before embarking. In adventure racing, as part of the competition, this is done during your race to test your ability in this discipline as well as the endurance sport disciplines.

One of the variables common in adventure racing, that I do not usually include in my multisports, is being linked together with a teammate. I often had to run connected to a teammate with a large rubber workout band or run and bike connected by a rope, where one teammate would run through forested trails and the other would mountain bike for a leg with each being tied together by a short string. Swim sections often called for staying within a maximum distance of a teammate. This was a common challenge race directors would throw in amidst the other sport elaborations to further test competitors.

While my love for multisport began with my triathlon base, it grew with adventure racing. I liked the wild, outdoor element. I learned new disciplines and new skills. In addition to running, biking, and swimming, I added more off-road versions of these sports plus paddling, navigation, and rappelling skills to my backcountry knowledge from being in the mountains. Adventure racing is a great way to study, learn, and practice how to build your own multisport.

Before I embarked on around-the-world multidisciplinary adventures like sky running ultras, big summit climbing, and then creating my own multisports, I began by expanding my sports base and knowledge with adventure racing.

I started adventure racing in the early 2000s. I was inspired by the Eco Challenge race that was televised in the 1990s. When I had the chance to compete locally and regionally, I jumped at it. While racing on- and off-road triathlons, I also competed in adventure racing distances from sprints, to mid-distances, to full-day events.

One such outing was the Eco Oklahoma Quartz Mountain Adventure Race, billed as a 12-hour race. This adventure started out cold in our team's hometown of Wichita, Kansas. It felt refreshing to be at home, not at work, outside at 9 AM on a

Friday, as I loaded our trailer with camping, navigating, racing, and general survival gear with my teammates. Greg, Mari, Jim, and Stan made a mixed-gender team of four and my dad and I made a mixed team of two. As we became acquainted and finished our loading, we drove several hours away to Oklahoma.

The Quartz Mountains stuck up off the Oklahoma plains like the cactus pokes on our legs we would all soon have. The pokes were better than the usual cramps and contusions I was left with from racing hard in the heat and minor crashes on the rocks with my mountain bike. Falls were inevitable. I always hoped they weren't serious. We checked in and set up camp, in an every-person-for-themself-kind of way. Somehow, despite the gear, food, and supplies needed for at least four sports, two nights of race-site camping, and fueling for a 12-hour or more adventure race through multiple terrains with hot and cold temperature fluctuations, we managed to be organized. I ended up with the executive suite of tents that I could easily stand in and have plenty of space to layout my stuff, which calmed me before an event.

In preparation for the next day's unknown challenges, we drove around the racing area to scope out the scenery and orientate ourselves for the race. It felt like we were in New Mexico or Arizona in the American Southwest, instead of Oklahoma. The mountains were craggy and beautiful, nestled against a solid blue lake. The browns, oranges and greens of fall were silhouetted in the sunset as we made our way into town for dinner. I was glad to have plenty of good fuel for the early morning start and one less thing to worry about pre-race, which was always a relief before any type of competition, event or climb.

Dinner helped our teams bond and we made a plan to work together to finish the race. I was used to the individual racing that triathlon brings, so it was a welcomed change to be around others to strategize and share our skills. Together we could go faster, farther, and navigate better, as long as we trusted each other and worked as a team.

The bright stars freckled the dark night as we rode back to camp. I was soon asleep in my spacious tent, with my cozy sleeping bag, over three layers, listening to the howling coyotes that surrounded the site by 11 PM.

The next morning started early and cold. My favorite nutrition bar at the time (I went through phases that lasted anywhere from a few months to years), that I settled on for breakfast, was too hard to eat; I just didn't have an appetite, as often happens before a big event. I was also feeling nervous about the dwindling amount of toilet paper in the bathroom. (This is normal and exactly why I always packed extra in my triathlon, adventure racing and multisport bags.) I tried to be as organized as I could, packing my racing backpack full of tested foods and topping off my hydration bladder with the ounces I would need for warm temperatures and lots of miles in the sun, as well as making sure my hat and sunscreen were applied, and my lightweight racing sunglasses were at the top of my pack for easy access before the pre-race meeting.

The Eco Oklahoma Quartz Mountain Adventure Race began with a three-mile run on a beautiful beach along the lake. It was shocking, as race starts always were, to feel the adrenaline mixed with excitement, fear, nerves, and glycogen, but again a treat to find myself waterside without having to travel to the ocean.

The four-team started fast and stayed fast as my team tried to keep up. We knew this would be a theme, as it is when you are competing with elite athletes, so we had mentally prepared to work for every inch and push our limits and comfort speed.

The run took us up sand hills and near the water. The sprint warmed me, and I was hot in my racing shorts and top. After the transition, we headed for the next leg: kayaking. Once again, my body was in a bit of shock switching from lower body power to upper body power, but the change of being on the water rather than just next to it made me happy and felt good. Our team shone on the kayak legs, and we were, for once, not chasing our teammates but instead leading the way. After this first lake crossing kayak, we ran through one of many cocklebur oceans. The almond-sized, light-to-dark brown cockleburs were a staple of adventure racing in the Midwest. These burs were covered with sticky points and attacked our shoes and knee-high gators with each step. Near this lake in particular, bushes numbered in the thousands, and we raced right through, getting covered in cockles as well as in their sandbur cousins.

The run took us up a road where we looked like a SWAT team, with the four team's matching white shirts, black pants, and our blue and yellow backpacks, all of us running up toward a house, full tilt in goldenrod tech hats. The neighborhood deposited us onto a mini mountain, where we had to hike, as fast as possible, up rocks, around trees, and through grass to a checkpoint at the top. We used our maps to make our own route to this checkpoint after exiting the water. I was breathing hard and grateful to reach the top, only to head back down at breakneck speed. We rushed back to our boats to paddle and navigate to our next checkpoint, around the bend, through the cockleburs and sandburs, up some rocks, punching our racing passport that assured the organizers we had completed the correct course and reached each checkpoint.

The next kayak was longer and lasted several hours, with our three boats, of two people each, staying close. Here we paddled to the modern conference center on Lake Altus-Lugert, also reminiscent of the Southwest with its National Park-style wood and timber design, where we parked the boats on the rocks, and ran the stairs to a checkpoint on the roof of a covered bridge. The last remaining checkpoint for this segment was another kayak away, but this one was on level ground. Once we acquired the control point, our navigation pointed us back to the beach.

I was sure things would get better as soon as we came to the next leg, a little idea I held onto throughout the race that never really proved itself. The promised comfort of the sport change up motivated me and gave me enough to hope.

Our next leg was mountain biking, and I knew we would be sprinting as soon as we hopped on the bikes. I was right. In the transition, I refueled, repacked for this new sport leg, and plotted our navigation points on our racing map. We each kept one in a waterproof case that could loop around our necks and that we could easily read while running, biking, and paddling, and not lose, or get lost ourselves, a grave and costly mistake. While multisporting wasn't a competition like adventure racing, having multiple map copies, course layouts, and notes about the locations of the day in waterproof cases for each participant and crew like these was a constant component.

We rode fast to a dirt road where we did have to walk our bikes at deep sandy areas that, dishearteningly, became unpassable via pedaling. It was frustrating to have to stop, but that is part of the unknown and challenge of adventure racing and in multisport. There will always be environmental hazards.

We made it into a tiny town where we had another twist: a mid-race scavenger hunt on the small streets, splitting up to find the items needed to continue our racing course. This added a nice diversion and was one of those elements of surprise included in adventure racing that you wouldn't find in a triathlon, but that you could create in your own multisport. The 15-mile ride went by quickly and soon enough we were back at the transition for another kayak across the lake to the conference center and a trekking (it ended up being mountain climbing) section.

Next, it was time for the start of the big, rocky mountain hikes. I moved as fast as I could and tried to avoid the plentiful cactus while navigating a path through the unmarked wildlife. The view from the top showcased the dense lake on one side and brown and green plots of farmland on the other. I caught my breath and helped navigate our path down. We continued through the rocky, vegetative terrain following the ridgeline in pursuit of the checkpoints. We found the two up top and the next one in an endless ravine full of rocks that we haphazardly followed all the way down to a dry creek bed and the ROAD—flat land! I was relieved. Then we resumed our sprint pace. We reached the next point by climbing up the side of the dam, which was one of the things I loved most about adventure racing. The adventure! The discovery! The finding of new paths and exploring new areas in unexpected ways. Then, we had two more mountains to climb. The first one went like the previous ones, but it was dark by the time we arrived at the second one. The hardest part was coming down over the big rocks. With the limited visibility of nighttime, maneuvering over the rocky terrain became even more challenging as we rock-hopped through the boulder fields.

In the dark, we made our way to the last checkpoint: a cave. It was exciting seeing what might be the much-talked-about cave challenge on our topographical map, and we were all thrilled to reach such a specialty control point. Oddly enough, it was only 200 meters away on a marked trail, but we had the hardest time finding it in the pitch-black narrow canyon area surrounded by brush and trees.

In adventure racing, we would not be able to move forward until we found each checkpoint at each point in the race. If it took us longer, we could lose valuable time that would put us behind in the competition. Our team had to be competent in not just the endurance sports and extra surprise challenges, but in finding the best direction in which to proceed.

In multisport, I more often found myself up against self- or life-imposed time constraints, such as needing to be back for an event or commitment, running low on water or fuel, or racing against the setting sun, opposed to the time restraints of a race with other competitors in an adventure race or triathlon.

On this day, it was then home free on a final kayak across the lake. Eerie at first, once I settled in, it was peaceful on the water in the dark. I focused on the flashing light on the far side of the lake, since that was the only thing I could see to navigate with. I enjoyed the kayaking the best because my comfort on the water, and I felt like we could do it well and hold our own in the boat, as opposed to chasing everyone on land. After the paddling leg, back on solid ground, I sprinted to the finish in the dark, 12 hours in, with my teammates.

As is often true in extreme racing, or intense multisport days, as soon as we stopped, I felt better. As usual, it feels like it all just suddenly ends, instead of the real 12 hours and 28 minutes I spent looking forward to that moment.

My recovery consisted of showering at the campground, an added luxury, if spartan, bundling up, and gulping down some packed-ahead orzo salad along with other assorted food items.

The six of us gathered around our campsite talking, full of endorphins, before heading to bed in our tents and vehicles. But we didn't sleep. Our bodies were either too full of adrenaline or too tired. Then the wind started howling and it began raining. When you are in a tent, even a breeze is noisy, and a sprinkle feels like a rainstorm. It was another classic night of camping out and not sleeping with the post-racing adventure replay in my mind.

I had wonderful memories of backpacking as a child, until the overnights in a tent. Nights could be long on the mountain. Sleeping bags liked to slide downhill on even the slightest decline and food often turned to ill-tasting mush with high-altitude cooking. I had also slept quickly and deeply when camping, exhausted from the day and desperate for repose. Either way, tent life, even with a few added comforts of a campsite, was part of the adventure, even after the race stopped.

Adventure racing experiences like these, that required multiple disciplines, sports, and skills, set me up to have the base knowledge of multisport and multisport concepts. Being in a new place and exploring different areas by my own engine fed my love of the outdoors and travel with purpose. Training for adventure racing sports and the sports of triathlon helped me become a multidisciplinary international athlete. I had some more life experience to get under my belt, but the seeds of the new multisport were planted.

The New Multisport

In delving into the world of triathlon, its variations, and roots, as well as into adventure racing, we can see where multisport originates and how it starts to differ.

We have progressed from three sports, and variations of those, into the adventure racing additions of paddling sports, ropes skills like rock climbing and rappelling, navigation, and even surprise challenges.

After traveling around the world climbing mountains, running volcanoes, trekking deserts, hiking canyons, bush-whacking jungles, swimming seas, and paddling oceans, I wanted a way to integrate these disciplines into my life as well. I wanted to do them on a weekly level, and not just as something I trained for and competed in several times a year or over a season.

I wanted to expand the realms of my triathlon and adventure racing background to now include even more sports like mountain climbing, ultrarunning, marathon swimming, new ways of paddling using packrafts and stand up paddleboards, gravel biking, and more fringe sports that sometimes popped up in adventure racing like inline skating, scooters, and roller skis, but that were not widely featured.

I wanted to combine them and make my own human-powered routes and integrations where I lived. I no longer wanted to be limited by a preset race that followed someone else's ideas, timeline and destination. My goal was to create my own and share this movement that was happening in the world of extreme sports and extreme distances at a doable and approachable level, where you could go as short or a long as you wanted in your own singular way.

Now with the principles outlined in *Go Multisport*, you don't have to be a professional, elite level, record-breaking athlete to participate in self-propelled travel. You don't even have to go around the world or travel to some faraway place. By going places via created trails no one had ever linked or combined before, I was on the forefront of the multisport world and leading exploration in my regional area, which is what the new multisport is all about.

Instead of the combo of two or even three sports, we can add more sports to make bigger and bigger combinations that take more and more preparation and work, but that offer better rewards, mentally from the challenge of building the routes and linking them all together, and physically, offering longer and more distance- and skill-based challenges.

The new multisport is not about being the best, winning, or even being fast. The new multisport is about staying fit and testing our own limits. The new multisport isn't a race, like a triathlon or an adventure race, or even an ultramarathon. Instead, it is something that is more sustainable and more enjoyable. It is something we can do on the weekends and using the environment around us. Multisport is now the opposite of an official event. We can do it with family and friends and define what success means to us as we go. If we are being challenged, having fun, and exploring, that is what makes this new multisport successful.

I wanted a way to combine my love of multisport to go out and have fun, but still be challenged. My goal was to continue to train for mountain climbing, ultrarunning, and distance swimming, among other sports simultaneously, but in a whole new way. I had years of experience running fast. It was now time to run happy. I was ready to swim, climb, hike, kayak, bike, SUP, ski, and pack happy, all via multisport.

For short range adventures, I rode my bike to the YMCA, swam in the pool, and rode my bike home. I ran to the pool and ran home, throwing in a stand up paddleboard on the river by my house before and a kayak after. Living between two rivers has advantages. I biked to the neighborhood pool for outdoor lap swimming in the summer or walked with the baby in the adventure stroller, alternating lap swimming and child tending with my husband while on parental leave. I ran to the gym in the morning, lifted weights, and ran home. I biked there for group fitness class and biked back. I ran to my family home, hopped in the pool for an outdoor water weights resistance workout, and ran back to my own home feeling cool and ready to tackle the next few miles.

I wasn't doing these combination workouts for training. Typically, in triathlon prep, brick workouts are popular. For example, a I might train with a bike/run or swim/bike. Instead of making training a focus of my multisport workouts, I was doing them for fun. They allowed me to be creative by using the resources I had to design workouts that fit my exact situation, season and mood. Multisport fueled my deep human desire to create and be active in the great outdoors.

I didn't have to race. I could race or train for a race if I wanted to, but multisport put the joy in the movement itself. Multisport celebrated doing something I liked to do—outdoor endurance sports—because they brought happiness and fulfillment to my life. Multisport let me participate in movement for its own sake and not only for competition.

It also added an element of unexpected challenge to my otherwise normal workouts. The challenge of additional sports kept me energized and looking forward to the newness ahead.

For mid-range options, I biked to yoga with my yoga mat strapped to my back, did hot yoga for an hour, and biked home while cooling off in the Kansas wind. My favorite combination might be running to the lake I swim-train in on a hot summer morning. This links my two favorite sports together and solves the problem of how I get from here to there. As the humidity pulls the week's toxins from my body, I am drenched in a cleansing sweat. Running down the dock and jumping into the cool green lake waters for a swim after this feels amazing and freeing. I can always run home or ask for a ride. I also love biking to the lake. The water's release is not quite as demanded as it is with an all-out power run, but the muscle tension that instantly disappears in the water and the weightlessness cannot be beat.

One of my favorite memories from college is during the final days of summer, when students returned to town before classes started. It was this blissful in-between time where we were busy getting ready for school, but not yet busy with school. The town still felt like a town on its own, with parents and families, and not yet like a college town, for a few more days. In the evening, I would run from my apartment by campus to the city park pool. There I would lap swim outside during the open swim hour. I would jump and dive off the diving board a few times before tucking my goggles into my swimsuit top, throwing back on some shorts and shoes, and running home to my apartment in time for dinner and class the next day. This option was only available to me on a few short days a year and it was one of my most treasured and enjoyed multisport workouts.

After 30 years of competing in endurance sports and living an adventurous life, I wanted something that would tie all my interests together. Multisport brought the endurance challenges of running, swimming, triathloning, adventure racing, paddling, and climbing mountains together under one umbrella. Even better, I could do them where I lived, at home, by walking out my front door. If had a lot of time, I could go far, like to the next state over or another country. If I didn't have much time, I could find sports around me using the time I had.

Read on to learn why, how, where, and when to use multisport in your own life and training. You can build your own by using your creativity and resources.

The possibilities are endless!

2 | Why Pursue Multisport?

Challenge motivates us. Challenge inspires and invigorates us. It instills confidence and satisfaction when we meet our goal. Integrating multisport concepts into daily life gave me more challenges that in turn made me happier and more fulfilled.

Exploring opens new worlds and new ways of thinking. It is one of my favorite things to do and multisport is one of my favorite ways to do it.

But why? What makes multisport such a unique and effective means of exploring your environment, your interests, and your own potential?

I have always had a drive for discovery. Creating multisport events and activities to participate in around my city, state, and region has fulfilled this drive in my own life. It has even taken me around the world.

By staying curious about new areas and modes of sport, I learned new skills. I developed a wide range of personal strengths through this discovery and learning of new things. Multisport brought continual new experiences through types, distances, challenges, and sport combos every year, every season, every month, every week, and even every day.

Perhaps the core reason of why to multisport is to explore the world around you by your own propulsion, awakening curiosity, and alleviating the boredom of modern life.

Let's be clear: the top reasons you should get into multisport are for fun, challenge and exploration. Yes, multisport also offers cross training and fitness longevity, but each of these things should act in service to bringing joy to your life and expanding your horizons.

Multisport as Cross Training

Multisport works for cross training by giving you new sports to try within your key sports training. Since I have such early triathlon beginnings, I think of my key sports as swimming, biking, and running. Perhaps you like to run. Maybe your key sport is biking or paddling, snowshoeing or skating on ice trails. By adding in multisport, you can cross-train your muscles in new ways to stay balanced and become stronger. It will also help you mentally as you try new activities in new situations and environments.

This added stimulation, both physical and mental, of multisport helps you be an athlete longer, giving you longevity in your sporting life. I have a goal of being a life-long athlete. Avoiding overuse injuries from overtraining in one sport area as a multiport athlete will help with this as you rotate sports. Mentally, new endurance sport varieties keep me wanting to be active and get out. I want to try new things and go new places with my fitness. Multisport allows me to do this.

The multisport movement is an investment in your long-term health. Staying active via multisport helps keep chronic illness at bay. The multisport lifestyle is a complete opposite from the modern day sedentary lifestyle. It is a fight back. It is an alternative path. It is freedom from the mundane, average and expected. Join the multisport movement and adapt it as a long-term lifestyle and habit. Doing so will prolong your years of being an athlete. Use multisport as part of your health strategy in the long run. Invest in the equipment, skills, and developed talent that multisport gives rather than in doctor visits and quick-fix reliance. The multisport movement gives you a choice and you can choose your health.

Trying and making new sports part of my fitness rotation is also F.U.N. *fun*! I Rollerbladed with inline skates in the 90s. When I wear mine now, it makes me feel like a kid again and brings back memories from that time in my life. Rollerblading is a diverting workout I can add to break up my biking and running. I can go faster than running but feel more freedom than biking. Similarly, stand up paddleboarding is a newer sport without youthful memories. By adding this event to my rotation and multisport days, I can try something from the 2010s, learn, and master it while being on the water, one of my loves, and paddling, another one of my core sports.

Multisport for Post-Injury Recovery

One of the key times the multisport concept and multisport lifestyle comes into play is when recovering from an injury. Is there an injured runner out there who has not been told to aqua jog in the deep-water pool as a tide over for an overuse flare up? I have done my share of aqua jogging, but multisport lets us put the goal of preventing injuries, especially overuse ones, at the forefront by including a variety of sports and elements in our training. By having a host of sports to choose from in your training arsenal, you don't have to run every day. You can rotate, you can combine, you can try new, and invent new. If you do end up fancying a jog in the deep water, which can be quite fun, let's make it part of a run/swim/aqua jog/water aerobics/water Zumba/yoga SUP/bike multisport to keep things exciting!

I learned that multisport can be a savior during pregnancy and postpartum recovery as well. These times in my life were full of restrictions. One thing about restrictions is that they allow you to be creative while coming up with ways to do what you want to do. Still wanting to be active through pregnancy, I used multisport combos to achieve longer endurance training when I couldn't solely run as far. I rotated through my roulette of sports, slowly letting go of each when it became time.

After my children were born, I made my way back to the water as soon as possible, but I added fins and paddling as I built back to running long distances. Multisport gave me a huge variety of ways to retrain and rebuild. I didn't have to be discouraged because I had so many options to choose from that all addressed different muscle and body systems in different ways.

Multisport as Exploration

Multisport gives you a reason and a way to explore locally. When I bike and run to my nearest lake to swim or do a winter stand up paddleboard, I am activating multidisciplinary thinking. Not only am I outside enjoying (or not on particularly rough weather days) nature, but I am also pushing my limits with endurance combinations that put me in nature itself.

I customize self-propelled transport adventures for miles in and around my city on routes I create, mixing up each sport in turn with weather, time, training, and destination in mind in all compass directions. By combining the elements of triathlon, I can make unique tri days swimming, biking, and running in new nearby locations. I can urban explore drainage and canal systems using the principals of urbex. As I link locales and sports together for multisport events, I create multidimensional outlets for running, biking, swimming, canoeing and other wheeled sports and elements from adventure racing. You can learn to do this too, all via multisport. Multisport gives us a reason to explore.

What's better, multisport is an all-weather, all-season activity. When it snows or gets icy I can snowshoe or cross country ski instead of running outside on slippery paths. I can also use those days as indoor pool training opportunities. Having a variety of winter sports to choose from and combine helps me lean into winter more.

From ice paddling, to icy outdoor plunge pools, to running on frozen rivers, multisport gave me an entire new set of sports to do in the winter that enlivened a challenging time of year. A bonus was that after running and boating in below freezing temperatures and frozen conditions for weeks on end in the winter, once spring set in, anything above 30 degrees felt balmy and fresh. Being a year-round outdoor multisport athlete made life outside more exciting.

Multisport Gets You Outside

By moving yourself through the great outdoors, you gain all the benefits of being in nature, like less anxiety, better sleep, increased focus, and boosted immunity. You can retreat to the woods for a stress-reducing forest bath while mountain biking or trail running or dive to the bottom of a sandy lake to experience being surrounded by mood-boosting teal waters on a swim hike. Multisport is multipurpose.

Spending time outdoors brings balance to your physical, mental, emotional and spiritual health. It is the original act of self-care. Learning how to thrive in the outdoors is a skill you develop by participating in multisport. You learn to spend alone time with yourself on long, human-powered journeys and develop relational skills as you embark on lasting, shared multisports with others on your team. Multisport gives you a reason, an excuse, and a way to spend at least 12 non-stop hours outside, reaping additional benefits beyond the multisport itself. Even if you only give yourself an hour of fresh air, you can still increase your contentment factor by detaching from modern life in the outside world.

Multisport Fits Your Life

Time, the elusive element for us all, is a friend of multisport. Multisport can take days, but it can also take as short as 30 minutes or an hour. The tenets of multisport want us to use what we have. When I was desperately short on time in the throes of new motherhood, I knew I could use multisport to fit in a stroller run combined with weights or yoga by following my multisport ideas.

Multisport is also a great way to help you finally get around to trying something new!

Training for long-distance multisport events or mastering new ones infuses your life with novelty. The change in fitness routines is sometimes exactly what the body needs to stay on the edge of peak performance and fitness. When I shock my body with new sport styles, I garner the best results. A winter snowshoe from a surprise snowstorm always leaves my leg muscles tired and my body hungry. The shock of adding something unfamiliar creates new ways for the body to adapt and work.

Multisport allows us to create and live an adventurous life without having to travel far from home. The reason for this is because multisport travels *with* you! When I do want to venture farther afield, I am more confident and have more geography skills to use when designing travels, trips, and integrating multisport into my voyage.

Use the list of individually powered endurance events and sports progressions (page 41) to alternate activities depending on your destination. Heading to Alaska with the family? Dog sled like the Iditarod. Hawaii for work? Outrigger canoe. Snowshoe or run and add a cold plunge or ocean swim and your day transforms into a multisport adventure. Stuck in a hotel? You can even multisport indoors when you must. Try a pool workout, followed by a weights workout in the hotel gym, followed by rowing on the erg. Then take advantage of the hot tub or local sights for beach hiking, trekking or coasteering. By doing so, you are adding to your personal development by staying curious and exploring and connecting wherever you are.

Multisport Helps Build Complete Health

Multisport unites my family, work and sporting life. This connection offers fulfilment and give us standout, special experiences. Focusing on experience has been shown to be more rewarding to humans versus buying and acquiring more stuff. When you live out the experience, you create a lasting, and in the case of multisport, empowering memory. These memories instill a sense of pride and offer self-esteem for all ages in the long run.

In the pages to come, you will see how I celebrate most of my birthdays with a multisport event. Long weekends and holidays are perfect occasions as well. By creating memories around multisport outings, I am empowered in new and different ways each year.

Multisport is also good for cognitive health. When we create, design, and develop multisport days, our brains feel happy. By making our own memorable multisport enhancements, we contribute to a fulfilling, healthy brain lifestyle.

Trying something new, like multisport, contributes to our overall cognitive health. When we create thought patterns, ideating different ways of thinking and doing things through multisport, our brains become more engaged.

By working with new patterns formed from multisport we help our brains achieve brain health balance. Experimenting, map reading, wayfinding, adjusting on the course, trying a new sport, adapting, collecting equipment, mastering a new skill, studying nutrition, learning wilderness areas, and navigating continental zones, are all part of developing multisport events that are also great for your brain.

It feels good to have power over your own health and fitness. Multisport is a way to continually do that through your different life phases. Multisport allows you to keep learning and challenging yourself on a mental plane as well as a physical one, no matter what phase of life you are in.

Multisport gives you a goal, a dream, something to work toward, and something to look forward to. It infuses your training with challenge and gives you something, an event, a day, a travel, a combo, to train for. Multisport is a coping mechanism for when life gets hard. You have something you can go out and do that makes you feel good, that feeds your soul, that nourishes and enriches your life, and that allows your body, as well as your brain, to stay active and engaged. Additionally, having a future focus frees you from feeling stuck in your life.

When you have a multisport planned, you can organize your life around that. It helps as you prioritize your to-dos and schedule on a daily, weekly, monthly, quarterly, seasonally and yearly basis.

Working multisport into your training with jobs, family, travel, children, and commitments is achievable thanks to multisport's fluid nature and ability to meet you where you are. I have a 15-year goal in the back of my mind. It has not been the right time in my life to reach it yet, but it is there, and when the time is right, I will be ready to work toward it. When I reach that next life phase, I can plan and train around that specific multisport goal that fits with my outside-of-sporting life commitments.

By having a future goal-multisport, you can train for that, adding challenge, fun and exploration along that way that boosts your mental fortitude and function.

3 | How to Create Your Multisport

When looking to create multisport events of your own, I recommend starting by building sport combinations around your current interests and skill sets, looking at endurance-based sports or those involving self-propulsion.

When you think about creating your own multisport, think about the combination of two to three sports, rooted in endurance, which will then be combined into one: that of multisport.

With my triathlon background, I usually always include a swim, a bike and/or a run. For longer multisport events, I like to run or swim first for either logistical ease or for required physical demands. I use biking to cross long distances. Trekking and hiking are other options for longer events where running is harder to maintain. I then usually add a paddling sport from adventure racing that fits the needs and location of the day. Everything else pops in as the event and conditions demand, which we will see in more future examples.

When we combine events in multisport that we rotate and segue through, we spread the muscle work to different focus areas of our bodies, and the mental work is spiced by that variety, which allows us to go farther and longer in multiple arenas. This is one of the secrets of triathlon, adventure racing, and now of course multisport. More sports equal more fun and more ways to cover distances!

Each of these can help you choose your own version of sport for each multisport you do.

One of my favorite things is finding new ways to make human-powered, wheeled adventure and finding transport devices to add to the following sports repertoire and sport progressions.

I organize my multisport into the traditional adventure racing six category framework that includes Paddling, Wheels, Animal Friends, Catching Air, Covering Terrain and Ropes (see page 41 for a full list). These categories give your sporting a structure and a reasoning. However, there are always new ideas and iterations to try, so this list of sport ideas is ongoing and serves simply as a guideline. I encourage you to find your own human-generated sports to add to this list, and please, share them with me. I love to find new things!

MULTISPORT

EXAMPLES & CATEGORIES

Paddling Sports

Canoe

Cataraft

Flatwater Kayak

Ice Paddle

Ocean Kayak

Outrigger Canoe

Packraft

Paddle Boat

Pedal Boat

Pedal Kayak

Raft

Row

Stand Up Paddleboard

Surfski

Whitewater Kayak

Wheels Sports

Aqua Tricycle

Cyclocross

Elliptical Bike

Fat Tire Snow Bike

Gravel Bike

Hand Car

Hand Cycling

Hydro Bike

Inline Skate

Mountain Bike

Multi-Person Bike

Rail Bike

Recumbent Bike

Recumbent Trike

Road Bike

Roller Skate

Roller Ski

Scooter

Skateboard

Stroller

Taga Bike

Tandem Bike

Trike

Unicycle

Animal Friends Sports

Bikejor

Camel Ride

Canicross

Dog Scooter

Dog Skateboard

Dog Sled

Dog Sulky

Horseback Ride

Skijor

Catching Air Sports

Base Jump

Kiteboard

Kitefoil

Hanglide

Hot Air Balloon

Parachute

Paraglide

Pronefoil

Ice Sail

Ice Skate Sail

Sail

Skate Sail

Ski Sail

Snowkite

SUPfoil

Surfoil

Wakefoil

Waterfoil Bike

Windfoil

Wind SUP

Windsurf

Wingfoil

Whike

Covering Terrain Sports

Aqua Jog	River Board
Bike Surf	Rogaine
Boogie Board	Run
Boulder	Seabike
Canyoneer	Scooter Surf
Cave	Scuba
Crawl	Sit Ski
Climb	Skate Ski
Coastateer	Ski
Cross Country Ski	Ski Bike
Dive	SkiMo
Downhill Ski	SkiShoe
Finswim	Sled
Freedive	Slide
Hike	Snorkel
Ice Bike	Snowboard
Ice Dive	Snowshoe
Ice Swim	Stand Up Pedal Board
Ice Skate	Stilts
Jump	Surf
Monoski	Swim
Obstacle	Trek
Orienteer	Tube
Parkour	Walk
Prone Board	Urbex
Pogo	Zorbe

Ropes Sports

Abseil	Rock Climb
Archery	Shoot
Bungee Jump	Slack Line
Ice Climb	Tightrope
Mountaineer	Via Ferrata
Rappel	Zipline

Building Your Multisport

These sports serve as the base you need to build your own multisport adventure. This list represents many of the sports I have tried and many I still want to try. Primarily, they are human-generated individual sports that cover distance or incorporate those factors. You can also employ the multiuse idea for multisport in your daily life or for distanced-based multisport events.

Multisport is Multiuse

While there are exceptions, my definition of multisport is ultimately focused on **human-powered, endurance-based sports**. Happily, even with this, the six categories above give us a wide variety of options to choose from! (However, you should also look to your interests to add components that can complement your own adventure racing-inspired multisport.)

What lies at the heart of every multisport I come up with is that same spirit of the unexpected that defines adventure racing. Take obstacle challenges like rope climbs, wall scales, and crawls through mud pits or even puzzle solving, snorkeling for tokens in a mud-black pond, or a scavenger hunt inserted into the middle of a trekking section. We have all seen these types of challenges included in reality and extreme challenge shows. This element of the unknown, of chance, of focusing away from solely the physical, but adding in mental and arbitrary change, ups the ante and the drama of the day. That is why we welcome these types of anomalies into our multisporting escapades.

Team Multisports

What about team sports? Since they are not covering a distance, they are not typically listed. However, if you wanted to bike to a dodgeball game, play, and bike home that would be an excellent inclusion of multisport at a daily life level. This is an example of using the ideas and theories behind multisport to incorporate it into your life. Create a multisport event or create multisport options around events you are already doing. This every day, ground-floor level is encouraged in multisport.

These deviances from endurance can pepper your multisport, but I do like to stick with a core sport as a base and build pops of irregularity around that. The concept of multiuse in multisport adds an element of quirk that can enliven the tedium of long-distance endurance.

Animals in Multisport

"Beasts of Burden" is a term used in adventure racing for including animals in your multisport. Throughout history, animals have helped humans cover long distances and both horseback riding and camel riding are key components of multi-day, international adventure races. Camels are especially helpful in desert crossings with their specialized physiology, as are sled dogs in the arctic.

These animal inclusions in adventure racing, and multisport, also play up that element of chance, as competitors must practice and train their animal-handling skills and riding styles to succeed in these arenas.

Pentathlon includes equestrian. In this spirit, if the animal is helping you in some way with transport, it can be included in multisport. This allows us to also include burro racing among the animal section as a sidenote. Pack burro racing is recognized in Colorado as a heritage sport that commemorates the state's mining history and the role the burros played in transporting supplies. Why not add a running with a burro section to your Colorado mountain climbing, river surfing, downhill skiing, whitewater rafting multisport days?

As a Siberian husky mom, I become especially excited about incorporating huskies, sled dogs, and athletic canines into my multisport days. Anyone with a husky knows that life with one is full of endless energy and demands. We have learned that is just the elixir a well-balanced multisport calls for: high energy, curiosity, and demanding adventure into the unknown. Sports like canicross, running with a canine, bikejoring, biking with a canine, skijoring, skiing with a canine, and dog scooter, skateboard, sled, and sulky cart are all invigorating ways to get your four-legged fur friends active in your multisport days. They use training tools that sled dogs use in the on- and off-seasons. Use these tools too for urban mushing at home. You can even use your dog to help pull your stroller—with human supervision.

Having a holistic approach to multisport enables you to have a structure, but to be flexible within that structure.

Sport Progressions

Multisport also encourages us to try new versions of sport, expanding our thinking and ways of being active. Use multisport to find wonderous new iterations and thrilling new challenges.

Multisport allows you to be a progressive athlete. It gives you more ways to be a swimmer, a biker, a runner, a paddler, and beyond that grow with you as you progress as an athlete.

When we talk about being a swimmer, for example, there are many ways of participating in that sport category. Swimming is something you can do from a young age to an old age, and in a host of locations and forms. I have three wetsuits for at least three different types of swimming!

I have my original triathlon wetsuit that is full leg and sleeveless for U.S. lake swimming. I have my swimrun wetsuit that started off as full arms and legs that I then cut off at a swimrun event minutes before the competition start in the cold waters of the Baltic Sea. I can use it today for combination events and swimming in mildly cold bodies of water. I also have a high-tech, full-body, tight-fitting wetsuit that I used for some the coldest ocean water I have raced in. If I wanted to include surfing, rafting, SUP, or freediving events, I might have even more wetsuit versions.

These three different wetsuits represent three different ways to be a swimmer, plus more. These three alone include triathlon swimming, adventure racing swims, often done in ill-fitting

PFDs, swimrunning, multisport swimming, open-water swimming, distance swimming, marathon swimming, around the world classic swimming like crossing the Dardanelles Strait, and cold water swimming. My swim gear tubs hold even more versions through the years, including age group racing, college club and rec league meets, water polo caps for days spent cross training with that sport, synchronized swimming practice in the summer, bifins and monofins for freediving, and all the accessories . . . the list goes on.

One sport alone holds so many progressions and versions when viewed through the lens of a multisport lifestyle. I can be a swimmer my whole life, but I can be a swimmer in different ways every few years with the variety and novelty multisport offeres. I love that with multisport, I can keep finding new ways to be a lifelong swimmer.

Getting Started

An easy way to get started making multisport combinations is to work through your own sport progression. This section shows how to expand your view on how to participate in your choice of sport or sports to broaden the fun, challenge, and exploration opportunities in your life. Find where you are on the list, for example, if you are a runner or a sailor, find that on the list below, and move on to the next item for an idea of where to start, what do next, and how to progress, or pick and choose what interests you. Use each of these ideas to try, test, combine, and expand upon for an entry point into this emergent multisport movement in the world of sport.

Progressions List

Running

Track
Cross Country
Road Running
    Half Mile
    1 Mile
    2 Mile
    3 Mile
    4 Mile
    5 Mile
    10k
    10 Mile
    Half Marathon
    Marathon
Trail Running
Triathlon
Off-Road Triathlon
Relay Running
Ultramarathon
Mountain Sky Running
Stage Race
Multi-Day Race

Swimming

Pool
Open Water

Pond
Canal
Lock
Lake
River
Ocean
Isthmus
Archipelago
Circumnavigation
Distance
Marathon
Swimrun
Cross Country
Ice Swim
Finswim
Freedive
Snorkel
Scuba
Underwater Orienteer
Water Obstacles
Water Fitness

Biking

Road
Mountain
Gravel
Snow
Adventure Race

Aqua Version
Bikepack

Paddling

Canoe
Kayak
Row
Raft
Packraft
Outrigger
Sail
Ice Paddle

Snow

Snowshoe
Cross Country Ski
Skate Ski
SkiMo

Now that we know what sports to use in multisport, as well as a few versions and types of these sports to work through, we can look at the tools we need to build multiport events and days. The tools you need consist of gear, what you can dream up, and your team of logistics support. You can start this process by defining your systems for each sport that will make up your multisport repertoire and outfit your adventure.

Systems

The number one key to a successful multisport is **systems**. If you are already an athlete, you have your system for your sport down. You know what you need for a run or a swim or a bike. If you haven't participated in an event you want to add to your multisport, you should train with that event first to nail down your systems for it.

For example, when I wanted to add roller skiing to a multisport birthday event, I first researched what other roller skiers were wearing. Then I practiced in roller skiing gear, as well as learning the new-to-me-sport, so that when it came time to integrate it into a combo, I didn't have to think about what kinds of gear to wear. I knew I needed a helmet, gloves, thick boot socks, and sunglasses.

Also keep in mind transitions. Transitions are a huge factor in traditional triathlon. They are a large success factor in adventure racing and multisport as well. Defined, practiced transitions between each sport segment allow you to have a well-oiled, fast-functioning, and strong-flowing multisport.

Nail down your sport, especially if it is new, your transitions, or lack of if you are keeping sports fluid, and your systems.

Your systems consist of personal gear, equipment, food and hydration, safety, communication, route finding, and backups for everything.

Personal Gear

Personal gear is what you are wearing. Each sport requires its own take on how to be comfortable when going a long way, often in wet, muddy, adverse weather, and away from the comforts of home. I like to wear a looser top and tighter shorts, but not tight pants. I have learned this from hours spent not just running, but hours spent running and biking. The same goes for swimming. You might want to swim in something different than a swimsuit if you know you will be biking to your swim site or running after.

The best way to design your personal gear systems is to practice. Know what you like for your individual sport and know what you like for the combo, even if you do a shorter version to test gear and practice. Think of everything from underwear to socks. I use a head-to-toe visualization technique for each sport and each transition thinking of my personal gear from top to bottom.

During peak training zones, I zero in on my personal gear choices, often wearing the same thing each week. I have a go-to outfit for my mid-week run and a go-to outfit for my long weekend run. This takes the stress out of thinking about my gear for my most important workouts. I have set options for each season that make getting out the door and going easier and accomplishable.

When training and racing without the ability to travel home or become clean with a shower quickly after, keep in mind long-term comfort for your gear as well as layers. For mid-day paddling between kid activities, I designed a base layer that could be worn all day with paddle equipment quickly added on and taken back off at the designated time. This also works for backpacking with and without children.

Your base attire should be something that can go the distance and stand up to long days and nights of multiple activities and temperatures. Getting clean might often be a long way off and you want to be as comfortable as you can be in the meantime.

Equipment

The obvious equipment is a bike, a boat, skis, or a scooter. Equipment also includes goggles, a swim cap (or several if you are swimming in cold water), specialized boots or shoes, helmets, and anything extra you need to wear on your person like a backpack, paddles, or blades outside of your personal clothing.

If you are hesitant about investing in a new piece of pricy equipment, try borrowing an item first to test, or purchasing a lower-priced used item, like a kayak, for example. Thank you to the dear friends who let me borrow packs, parkas, double boots, and ice axes to test my hand at mountain climbing, before making a full commitment to that and other similar gear-heavy endeavors.

Equipment can be acquired over time. You can start with the basics, like a bike, and build over the seasons from there. Consider it a long-term investment in your overall health. Yes, gear and equipment cost money, but since you are the engine, all your gear does not equal the cost of even one external motor piece like a speed boat, jet ski, motorcycle or camper. These recreational items have their value and might even be used to assist in multisport outings, like an RV support wagon on coast-to-coast events, but in terms of cost to play, multisport is a more economical recreational activity as it is self-propelled. By investing in multiport gear, you are investing in you, the engine, and your overall healthy lifestyle goals.

Having a set bag, satchel, or stuff sack that you keep your gear in during your training season takes the stress out of completely re-packing after each session (other than fresh top offs for clean items and fuel).

On that note, establishing a specialized area in your home, garage, basement, mudroom, or gear room for your bag to go also makes training goals achievable. It takes the guesswork out of each session as to where your needed equipment is. This goes for having a designated space in your garage as well for each item. When you know that every week your kayak goes here, your bike goes here, your paddles go here, and your fleet of strollers goes here, you can focus on the workout and less on where your equipment is when you need it.

Keeping equipment organized is the first step. Make a note of what needs attention or work after you finish a training session and add that to your multisport preparations. Always start reviewing equipment and gear in plenty of time before a multisport event is scheduled. That way if something does need repairs, patching, or fixing, you will have time to attend to it, and you won't be caught unprepared the night before a multisport day, or even worse, the morning of. Always pack and set out as much gear and equipment as you can before event day. To be extra safe, having multiples of items can act as an added precaution.

Keeping that equipment clean and in working order is its own full-time job that also needs attendance. My best advice for this? Make the purchase of a headlamp, as often work on this will need to be done late at night, when the children are in bed, in the off hours.

Speaking of off hours, I recently had to devote several while gearing up for a 100-mile expedition. I first created a personal gear and equipment list then proceeded to gather that gear from around my house, garages and storage areas.

There were so many sports! The fins were on top of the packraft that was on top of the military-grade SUP drybag. The packraft paddles and bag were on top of the handcrafted plyometric jumping box that was next to one of the strollers. I pulled warm foot liners from my cold water swimming storage bin and headlamps and batteries from my ultrarunning gear pile.

I dug out my mountaineering survival essentials from the bottom of a child carrier backpack as well as a partially full bladder from a trip I had done over six months before. That would need a good washing. I set it next to my other hydration bladders that ranged from an insulated version I used on top of some of the highest mountains of the world, to smaller, older versions I had stuffed in a first-generation Camelback, for its early simplicity, to use on wild lake crossings and swimrun combinations.

Then I pulled out a dry bag that had been stored in a kayak hatch to access, evaluate, and test the specific gear that I would need for this endeavor. "How fun! Look at the life I was living through multisport," I thought. Seeing all this gear and equipment that I acquired through my multisport lifestyle fueled my imagination and ignited a spark. I was built for exploration and going into the world by my own propulsion. It took a little bit of preparation and training, but that was all part of the fun and challenge.

Then I opened the drybag. It was covered in mold as I had left a nutrition bar in there too long among the dampness that also rusted my backup river knife and wetted my ever-dry emergency matches. Boat patch stuck to everything. Its storage bag had disintegrated, and the stickiness was doing its job from the inside. After a soaping and time in the sun, I repacked my drybag, trying to use what I already had.

One final review of the sand gaiters and snow models of the same, over the snowshoes, and roller skates and roller skis, beyond the child stroller's ski attachments and overflowing accessories bin, beyond the mass of backpacks and water resistant (always a must) bags, past the climbing harnesses, hiking poles, three types of helmets, various water shoes, scooters, beach tent (in the shopping cart), and mountain board, I was ready to go out. In any condition. In a multitude of ways and means. The multisport revolution was calling for me.

Food & Hydration

Testing is once again crucial when designing food and hydration systems for multisport. A one-hour multisport event will call for different fueling than a two to five-hour event, as will a 12-hour or multiple day multisport.

Develop a collection of foods, waters, electrolytes, and supplements, like amino acids and vitamins, that you like and enjoy to fuel your multisport.

I have found that mountain climbing calls for different fueling for me than ultrarunning as does paddling. I need to eat less dense and chewable food when running. When climbing I can do more chewing, but only up until high altitudes. Likewise, I have learned that during paddling, I can handle a snack like a sandwich, but only when I am stopped because I don't have use of my hands if they are on a paddle, and if I have enough water and it is not too warm of a day, making me extra thirsty.

I love a hydration bladder for easy-access fuel, but once again, in a boat I find I also like a hand-held bottle. I also use these at transitions for a drink change up, and to splash on myself when out in hot weather.

The best way to learn your fueling needs is trial and error. Sticking with a collection of items you like and enjoy will help you stay motivated to keep up with your food and hydration needs and can also serve as something to look forward to at your checkpoints and transitions.

If you plan to stop at gas stations, shops, or stores along your way, have money with you, and plan to buy on-the-go as another mode of discovery and exploration.

You will also want to establish a fueling system for before and after your multisport days and training.

When I was embarking on an intense three-month ramp up of paddling, I created a fueling system around my training. Saturdays were long run cardio building days, and I liked to eat my favorite burrito bowl for lunch after my big runs to replenish my body with nutritious food that I liked, enjoyed, and fueled me for the weekend kidtivities and chores ahead. I also established a set food routine for Sunday nights after long paddles. I knew I would be hungry and busy with family preparations for the week.

The best recipe for long-term training success was to create an easy, go-to meal to have each week that took the stress and guesswork out of that high-energy day for those months of training. I could set and control this variable to allow me to be flexible with any other variables that fired my way. I made a framework to work within to allow me to focus more energy on training and less on daily decisions.

I use this aspect of routine and control for hard training periodization during the year. I love variety too much to live by it completely, but it works for temporary actions you take to reach your long-term multisport goals.

Safety

One of the beauties of multisport is that it takes you away from civilization. This is why safety is an important part of your multisport systems.

Before embarking on your multisport adventure of the day, make sure to let someone know where you are going, have a phone, money, emergency gear, like a rain jacket, hat and gloves, and your sports version of the 10 essentials. For example, paddling will have a different set of the 10 essentials than hiking will, such as a tow rope, PFD, and lighting, per Coast Guard rules. Some of these might overlap, such as an emergency blanket, bivouac sack, whistle, or signal mirror.

Study what each sport and each area you are venturing into calls for when it comes to safety needs.

Once again, this is why it is important to try out and become comfortable with each sport in your multisport combo to learn, develop, and acquire the safety gear, along with personal items and equipment.

Communication

If you have a support team, or even team members at home awaiting your return, finding a way to communicate while on your multisport adventure is part of being prepared.

Think beyond the basic cell phone for instances when batteries and signals fail. Hand-held radios, walkie talkies, checkpoints, swag wagons, transitions, meet ups, drop zones, and signaling can all be part of your ground team communication planning.

Route Finding

One of my favorite parts of multisport is route finding and route creating.

A local travel atlas as well as trail maps can serve as inspiration for making routes for your multisport. National and state parks and existing trails can often be known starting points to inspire your planning.

Make sure that you identify a route and have a plan that you share with others before taking off. Then, if you want to freestyle or deviate along the way, you are doing so within known safety zones. Part of the fun is zigzagging and jagging when you feel led by nature, its surprises, and your specific surroundings.

Backups

Learn how each part of your gear and equipment works. Your gear breaking or malfunctioning is an eventuality. Have backups with you or waiting for you at checkpoints so you can work through gear issues to keep going with your multisport event. Backups for food and water are important too. Always have more than you think you will need, keeping in mind pre- and post-fueling and sharing with others who might need some along the way.

I like knowing that I have redundancies waiting for me in a drop bag on the course or at a support crew checkpoint. These redundancies lead to success. You never know when you will lose a shoe in the river, not to mention a paddle, or even a boat.

Once you have your list of sports and progressions to pick from, choosing what interests and appeals to you and your training, you know why and how to build your event, your systems are developed, practiced and ready to be implemented, and you have added in a few unexpected elements of surprise, you are ready to go!

So . . . where exactly *do* you multisport? Better question: why go anywhere? In this next chapter, I have prepped a few more stories and ideas on how to create multisport adventures using just the natural resources around you and sports from our six-category adventure framework, sports progressions list, and the multiuse tenet.

4 | Where Can You Multisport?

The best thing about multisport is that you can customize based on what you have around you, making use of the resources and locales you have available. If you live near the mountains, use the mountains; if you live near the ocean, use the ocean. If you live near neither, use old railroad rail-to-trail beds, prairie rivers, native grasslands, and urban centers to create your own adventure. Explore where you are and use your natural elements to make your core sports more challenging and find added fun.

Your location and weather conditions inform your multisport choices. Since I live by two rivers, I usually start there when designing my multisport days. I enjoy following the natural contours in my area with my human-powered sports. Think about how you might unite your own mountains, lakes, and rivers with bikes, rafts, rails, packs, climbs and other adventure sports. Activate backcountry and front country for your multisport adventures, too.

Multisport is a great opportunity to flex your creativity. It taps into our innate need as humans to travel and traverse the land around us and create something from those experiences. Being on the move allows you to learn the meaning of distance and the gradual transition of landscapes. It gives you time for reflection. You connect with yourself and your world as you move through it by your own engine power.

You are the engine. You can go anywhere with multisport. Use it in your daily life to go from point A to point B and make you feel alive. Planning to play pickleball? Why not run there, skate, scooter, ski or kayak. One day on the river, I paddled by packed pickleball courts at the local center and decided that next time I would kayak to the courts, play a round, and kayak back home. Multisport should be used on special occasions, as we will learn more about, but it should also be used in your daily life.

So, the answer to the question where to multisport is . . . *everywhere.*

Designing Multisport for Urban Environments

When we think about how to multisport in urban environments, we first need to think about what we might find in an urban area.

One thing present in almost all urban centers, especially in a multisport opportunity-rich industrial corridor, is the railroad.

The main idea for multisporting here is to follow the train tracks. Where do they go, how do they align, what hidden areas of town, under or over, do they pass through? What a wonderful, built-in way to explore a path that already exists, but also one that you might never have followed, especially by your own propulsion. The railroad has long been a fundamental element in all my adventures. The railroads around my home come alive as I follow and trace them on foot, bike, blades, or other wheels, through new areas full of history, stories, and places that once were.

The railroads are the hidden powerhouse of our nation, in the background chugging and working. The trains, always there if you are out long enough, are a motif of my outdoor multisport life. I heard them in the water while I was lake swimming. I heard them paddling and saw them as I kayaked American rivers. I raced them biking under their bridges on cross-town urban adventures, and I taunted them as I ran over their rusting trestles on the outside of town. The trains lulled, comforted, and reminded me I was part of something greater traveling cross country.

Other prime areas for urban multisport include parking garages. They are great places to wear a pack and walk up and down to train for mountain climbing when you can't get to the mountains. They are even better to bike up (good training, again) and cruise fast down. Icy or snowy weather? Head to the parking garage to workout outside, but in a sheltered place as another good option.

Urban exploring often starts with walking alleyways and stairways, hiking your city, as you get to know its secrets. Running downtown, too, allows you to seek out what you want to further explore and link at a faster pace.

From there you can start to build a multisport that makes sense for what you want to see, do and connect.

My family has a history with ditches, canals, creeks and streams. We get in them. We follow them. We hike them. We run and paddle them and get covered in mud. Along with the railroads, they are the other secret corridors of a city or countryside. Everyone knows they are there, but they are out of view just enough to be forgotten.

Try navigating your own interurban creek or creeks. Start with a map, then plot your multisport route. Maybe you hike and packraft, depending on water levels. Deep water, if narrow, allows for paddling a packraft. Shallow water might call for hiking, as you tow your packraft in between sections as needed. Walking, trekking, and running are options here too, or any combination of these. Climb down into the deeply recessed, long-forgotten areas you might have missed before. Even bring your bike. I have! Hiking back up a steep creek slope and bushwhacking on a cross-town mission with a bike is even more fun, in multisport adventure terms.

The more you are out trekking, biking, scootering, blading, skateboarding, paddling, and running in and around urban centers, the more you will notice what you want to learn more about. Some of the ways I do this include reading books on local history and history specific to the area you live, studying old pictures and maps, and learning about old school names and locations, older neighborhoods, and how cities have evolved over time by using online tools and local newspaper articles. Researching the history of an area before you travel to it is useful as well, to look for ways to multisport in urban environments not your own. By getting up close, like you do when traveling by your own power, you can learn even more.

Some of the key elements of urban exploration (urbex) to keep an eye out for while doing this are box culverts. Especially ones that go under streets, or even better, under highways. Box culverts come in squares or circles and can be big enough to stand in. They are versatile precast concrete products and used for underpasses, tunnels, subways, bridges, stream culverts, storage, and for you to find passage in while multisporting in an urban environment. While you are in the industrial corridor area, look for the companies that are making them, too, as an added urban benefit. Anytime you find one, you should practice running through it. Or, if it is a small one, and you are up for some cave simulation training, crawl. Biking under a highway through one is an enjoyable way to urbex as well.

Bike, hike, walk, or run, but always keep your location safe and watch out for trespassing. Don't forget to run any stairs you see, like fire escapes, while you are out for overall cross training. All fences are considered scalable in urbex.

Find you own intercity fun with bridges, tunnels, storage yards, abandoned buildings, grain elevators, structures, towers, factories, train yards, monuments, graveyards, shipyards, scrap yards, tire dumps, sandpit mines and quarries. Even if all you do is look for these on a multisport bike portion through town, you are guaranteed an adventure.

Urban exploring is dangerous, and often unsanctioned, and that is its allure. Make it even better with your own rewarding multisport combo that you develop along the way.

Multisport Makes the Familiar, Unfamiliar

One winter, my river froze over. I had watched the weather and checked the ice; it was thick. But then I had an idea. What if I kayaked on the river with the ice? The forecast called for just enough sun and warmer temperatures to melt part of the ice.

So maybe, if I was lucky, conditions would be thin enough for a boat to cut through or a small flow to carve between the sheets. It could be so fun!

I asked some experts, made sure I had the right kind of boat, and started researching. After reading up on the sport of ice paddling, I acquired the right safety gear and piled on my layers from mountaineering and winter paddling neoprene for a cold morning ice paddle. Here was a new iteration, ice, of a familiar sport, paddling.

It was magical crashing through the different ice thicknesses and marveling at the sounds and texture. The hard ice made a tick sound, and the thinner, weaker ice made a tock sound as I broke through it with my hull and blades. I sliced through two sides of white and silver as I weaved my kayak through the ice sheet looking for leads. The narrow slits opened until I couldn't go any farther, coming upon a frozen unbreakable plane of ice where once I paddled freely through the flowing waters.

I was surrounded by an entire new world right outside my door. I was having a new experience in a familiar place just by trying something outside my normal routine. It was thrilling, scary and challenging. My husband Parker and I took advantage of the perfect mix of weather, ice thickness, cold paddle booties, mitts and layers, skills, and safety knowledge to try a new-to-us paddling sport, and it is now a part of my winter sports mix. Even better, I explored my local river in a new season in a new way, and I gained new skills as I learned about the history and elements regarding an iteration of a practiced sport. Each time we went out we learned something and experienced something new. The secret was showing up and going out. Multisport gave us a way to do this that kept us wanting more.

"Opportunistic Travel"

One of my favorite terms is "opportunistic feeder," ever since I heard it used to describe a fox and other similar mid-range predators who eat plants, meat, and a mix of whatever they happen upon, embracing their omnivore nature. (It also summarizes my Siberian husky's approach to eating and finding food. He is *always* happy to seek out new gustatory opportunities, whether it is kiwis and mangoes or leftover eggs.)

So, I decided to adopt this adaptability for my own purposes. By taking advantage of the opportunity in front of me, whatever it happened to be, I would be seizing the moment and living fully in it. (The definition is also a literal one; when multisporting, you learn to eat when you can and sleep when you can, because who knows when you will have another chance!)

Parlaying this opportunistic approach more to travel and multisport, I strive to integrate multisport into my travel opportunities for work, fun, leisure, vacation and family time. It is rare now that an opportunity to travel out of city, state, country, continent, and hemisphere doesn't involve me pursuing multisport in some way. When it comes to multisport, look at travel opportunistically, regardless of its original purpose.

One of the first times I tried stand up paddleboarding was in the Bahamas after dragging my mom, aunt, and cousin to a barre class, before we spent the afternoon at our resort's water park. I used the playground atmosphere for an obstacle course-like multisport workout while outside having fun in the tropical sun. I balanced on the floating lily pads holding onto overhead loops, climbed water rock walls, jumped off high dives, and slid down tubes. I used the jungle gym areas to play and work new muscles in different ways.

Not all vacations call for workouts, of course—especially not the cloistered insides of a damp gym, elipticizing type of work-out. But on a particularly relaxation-based week in America's Southeast coastal islands, I filled my days with beach-based workouts to take advantage of my time, energy, and environmental opportunities.

On Sunday, I ran six miles around the island to learn it and explore its trails. On Monday, I talked our group into going on a stand up paddleboard river tour with dolphins who popped and flipped right next to us. On Tuesday, I ran to the resort's lap pool, swam a mile outside under the summer sun, a novelty at home, and ran back, all in the middle of the day when I would usually be stuck inside working. On Wednesday, I ran another six miles sweating in the southern heat and humidity, exploring the opposite direction on the island.

Thursday, I took advantage of being right on the beach for a beach run to the pool (a path I had to create on my own) for dedicated lap swimming followed by a beach run back and a Tabata interval workout in the sand using my bodyweight for resistance. That afternoon I surfed with a group in the welcoming waves. Friday, I rented a touring bike and took my time biking around the island looking at the new developments and the ins and outs of the weaving paths, enjoying the creeping vines and lush vegetation for several hours before lunch, naps, and evening sunset beach walks as well as free ocean swimming and boogie boarding. Trying a locally based fun activity every day gave me structure and made me feel like I had accomplished something, while also learning the land and taking in the sights being active.

I followed this same routine years later, on an island off Honduras. I filled my relaxing vacation days with runs, swim-run combos, and hikes among the rolling green hills. I enjoyed learning my surroundings, acquiring a feel for the climate, and using the water, beaches, and jungle in the fullest way possible, even when the rest of my day included leisure snorkeling, more hiking, playing in the water, and beach and destination walking. I integrated multisport into my vacations and came away with a more fulfilling experience all around.

As an adventure racer, I was always looking for ways to horseback ride to keep my skills up-to-date. When I traveled to old Scottsdale in Arizona, I made sure to go horseback riding as it is part of the American Southwest culture and doing so there made it even more meaningful than only connecting with the horses. The same held true for Iceland as I rode Icelandic horses with their unique fifth gait over otherworldly terrain as the rain fell after competing in an endurance mountain running event. After an ultrarun across the Canary Islands, I took advantage of being near the Sahara Desert and rode a camel. Exhausted from racing the day before, camel riding sounded like a nice, few-hours-break, and I hoped to gain future camel handling skills for adventure racing that could always include an animal friend component. I wanted to be ready.

Most every vacation with me had a way of turning into a multisport vacation in one sport form or another. It could even be as simple as hiking local trails or trying a beach aqua tricycle when near a lagoon.

These are a few examples of how to use multisport when you travel to try new sports and sporting playoffs that are outside the normal realm of thinking. Travel gives you access to new models of sport, new variants of old sport, new environments, new people, and new challenges.

These are just a few ideas on places where you can explore multisport. The next chapter explores the other facet: *when* is it a good time to begin your multisport journey? (Spoiler: the beauty is you can start right now!)

5 | When to Start Multisporting

Multisport can be done any time at all! Multisport can be used as a weekend training tool. It can be done midweek, broken up into morning, evening, or noontime workouts. One of my *favorite* times to incorporate multisport is over long holiday weekends and for birthday celebrations.

I am always coming up with endurance birthday event ideas. I would frequently be training anyway, so why not build in a party with the training that had to be done? Even if it was only biking to have birthday ice cream and then biking home, the combination and the celebration made these mini multisport constructions exciting. Here are a few constructions that incorporate many of the sports we have covered so far to help inspire or get you started on your own journey to multisport.

My Last 24 Hours: Trekking, Mountain Biking & Kayaking

My first-ever shift away from a traditional race was a multisport day I designed. This custom multisport event was called My Last

24 Hours of Being 24. On the eve of my 25th birthday, I created a 24-hour adventure race to remember my last 24 hours of being 24. I wanted to compete in a 24-hour race, however, I couldn't find one that interested me and that fit my timeline and destination criteria. So, I decided to make my own 24-hour adventure race to compete in against time and myself.

My dad and I curated a local route close to home, to keep us within our timing dictates, that covered 80 miles. Those 80 miles included 50 miles of mountain biking on area paths and roads, 15 miles of kayaking on our two family rivers of the Arkansas—the Little Arkansas River and the Big Arkansas River—and a lake we were able to link to the rivers with some off-grid recon and grit, plus 15 miles of trekking, taking us south of town and then back to our city's center. The full days' worth of multisport included rain and thunderstorms at the midnight start, rapids and portaging on the rivers, and even one of my most-loved things to do—especially when out exploring—treasure hunting, while boating along the banks of my main rivers. I even suffered a concussion in the middle of this event while padding under a bridge. Luckily, I was able to stay focused and keep going, after a quick health reassessment, as is often the case in adventure racing multisport competitions.

This event took mountain biking, kayaking and distance trekking skills and several layers of planning. The number 24, for 24 hours and 24 years, also had meaning to me, and going non-stop for that long signified that I was a true adventure racer, able to go an entire day without rest or sleep all in the name of racing and adventure.

Duaquathon

The next year during my first marathon training, on my 26th birthday, I created a birthday multisport duaquathon, combining biking and running for the duathlon part and swimming plus these two sports for the aquathon portion. The basis of this self-created duaquathon event allowed me to celebrate my birthday with matching miles and factor-in my needed long-distance training.

My dad and I alternated running and biking every other mile to Cheney Lake, about 25 miles away, from my home base. One person ran while the other biked and then we switched. This allowed us to extend our endurance training farther by alternating sports. This alternation offered a mental and physical reprieve and built on my marathon distance training. A creative solution like alternating sports allowed me to run farther than I was ready for, but in a responsible, safe-training way.

This was a different application of the traditional bike-to-run duathlon, but still featured the bike/run combo. The bout offered around five hours of exercise, which is always good to gain when endurance building. We started early in the morning to beat the heat that emanated from the rolling blacktop road that took us through the countryside with no shade or breaks from the sun. As if that was not fun enough, for multisport spirits, I topped off the event with a one-mile lake swim in the refreshingly cold waters of a Midwest lake in May as a post run/bike duaquathon aqua birthday reward and 26 miles total for 26 years. My family joined me with our Siberian husky for a waterside picnic afterward, with my mom packing a sweet birthday dessert that added to the festive feel.

Ultrarun/Swim

A few years later, I was deep in ultrarunning and had my mileage high enough to run all the way to Cheney Lake, plus some. I ran 28 miles, over a marathon distance, and swam one mile when I arrived at the lake to celebrate 29 years. I called this multisport event: Running to Cheney: 29 Miles for 29 Years. I started at 3 AM, the best time for all multisport beginnings is often the middle of the night, to beat as much heat as possible on the sunny, open, asphalt road to the lake.

Marathon Swim & Roller Skate

On my 30th birthday, long past the thrill and challenge of running 30 miles at a time, from years of ultrarun training and racing at that distance and beyond, I swam three miles in open water. This, in itself, was not a multisport event. However, since I also added roller skating to celebrate this milestone birthday of mine, I decided to count it as so. This is an example of an out-there, creative multisport combination. Who says you can't swim three miles in a lake and roller skate to celebrate? No one. In multisport, you are only limited by your imagination.

Run & Zipline Obstacle

For my 31st birthday, I returned to running, running 31km and adding what I would call obstacle training gymnastics by jumping, ziplining and climbing in and out of a foam pit for a full-body workout at a trampoline park. In multisport, the essence is the combination, and these obstacles mirrored those encountered in adventure races.

Swimrun

For my 32nd birthday, I was in full-on swimrun training mode for an upcoming race in Stockholm.

The swimrun endurance sport was born in Scandinavia and combines my love for ultrarunning and marathon swimming. It offered a new, ultra-endurance way to combine sports and multisport. Training to swim and then run through Sweden's archipelago in the Baltic Sea, I started right at home by testing out the emerging multisport and its accompanying load of specialty cold-water gear.

After practicing lake swimming and running, one right after another, I built local swimrun routes using what I had around me to train. I lived in Kansas, so I had to research and be resourceful to find places to run and swim for mid-distances without the typical built-in natural resources that might have been available to me elsewhere.

One of these swimrun training workouts consisted of three hours of running, in the early morning rain, via bushwhacking and fence jumping, to lake one, where I swam across, and then ran to lake two, across a highway and through a river under bridge crossing. I swam across lake number two and then ran to lake three, down dirt roads and massive mud puddles before swimming across it. I remember this training day as a great time of just being wet and living life outside. Training for multisport gave me an opportunity to be wet, wild and free. I also invented an entirely new route that I could later set fastest known times on while I was out exploring the urban wilderness around me.

Running, Swimming, Kayaking & Mountain Biking

As I turned 33, I took it up a notch on my multisport birthdays, this time with four distinct disciplines.

For my 33rd birthday multisport, I ran 13 miles, swam one mile in a spring-cold lake, kayaked 18 miles back to my family home starting point, and mountain biked one mile, to round things off.

Preparations for this event started weeks before with physical training, but activity officially began the night before with:

Part 1: Ride bike and gear bag over to starting point at my parent's house on Friday night for my mom, the support crew, to help shuttle between sports and locations as needed.

Part 2: Wake up at 5 AM on Saturday and meet my dad at our midpoint bridge rendezvous marker to run 5 miles to our first lake.

Part 3: Swim one cold mile at the lake as the sun rises. I was clad in my full wetsuit and two swim caps, as this was early spring, and the water temperatures were still low.

Part 4: Run 8 miles to the kayak put-in at the Valley Center Little Arkansas River confluence point, which had been reconnoitered in the weeks leading up to event day. I was using the rivers and their confluences to plan, route-find and create around. Portage boat from roadway to waterway on self-designated portage path.

Part 5: Kayak 18 miles downriver to my parent's house along the banks of the Little Arkansas back in town.

Part 6: Bike one mile around the Riverside neighborhood for 33 miles total for Birthday 33 Multisport.

I topped this celebration off with a make-your-own bagel bar, commemorating with my family outside on the patio. I had started and ended at home, zeroing out any need for additional transportation and homing in on human-powered fun. It was rewarding to get four different sports and 33 miles in, all without having to travel!

Marathon Paddle

Not wanting to leave out birthday 34, I only exercised one sport this year. But it was a distance event, where I kayaked 34 miles for my 34th birthday. It was my longest continuous kayak at the time, and I was able to do it in my very own backyard along the Arkansas River Water Trail. Even better, I ended at the Arkansas River and Northern Big Ditch confluence point. I had run to the point many times over the years, and this matched up with the southern confluence of the two that I had linked on a winter day during ultrarun training. Now I had kayaked to that point. Linking these self-created paths together created a northernly and southerly confluence paring of the Arkansas River and Big Ditch, my city's flood prevention canal.

By building my kayaking endurance here, I set myself up for more distance kayaking in the future and the epic 35th birthday to come. I also continued to forge new trails and new ways of staying active outside via multisport.

Five for 35 Multisport: Running, Swimming, Gravel Biking, Kayaking & SUPing

Turning 35 was a milestone, and I needed some way to mark that milestone. Doing something big and memorable sports-wise was only natural for me at this point. But I needed a multisport event that was bigger, better, harder logistically and more challenging physically than I had done before. I wanted to combine five sports into one for a five-sport multisport event. In one day. At one time. I dreamed up the epic 5 for 35 that would include running, swimming, biking, kayaking and stand up paddleboarding. Not only would I have to be trained in each discipline to cover the distances, but I would also need space and place to perform the five distinct endurance sports.

Thanks to my dad's help coordinating logistics and locations, I was able to stay in Kansas and close to home to race all five modes in one long multisport day.

He and I started running through the old growth forests of Cross Timbers State Park, a two-hour drive from home, in a light rain that turned into an invigorating storm halfway through.

As I ran on a rolling wet trail, full of water crossings, I felt alive and one with the forest. I loved running through the mud and old hickory trees, getting soaked from top to bottom in a booming thunderstorm that was loud and frightening, but comforting as well. It reminded me of all the other times I had been out alone among nature, reliant on luck and grace to make it back to safety. Being in this old place, where the trees of the East meet the grasslands of the prairie West made me feel one with my environment. I felt like a wild original Kansan, exploring the area, albeit I was in a spandex running outfit with waterproof trail shoes I used for my swimrun race from Sweden. But maybe I was not so different from the Kansas settlers of old after all, with a few wardrobe holdouts from the Old Country.

Harkening back to a motherland, in another way, it was the day of Prince Harry and Meghan Markle's Royal Wedding. My mom baked us fresh lemon scones for breakfast that we ate while listening to the BBC broadcast of the wedding as we drove through the dark Flint Hills of Kansas on our way to Cross Timbers. Just because I was in the wilderness multisporting, didn't mean I had to neglect my cultural duties. These additional elements of a historic event and birthday celebrations added to the air of excitement as my family and support crew set off on our multisport adventure.

After running several wet miles with the music from the *Last of the Mohicans* movie soundtrack in my head—original trail running music, we called it—I was properly warmed up for my next leg. We had reached Toronto Lake by then, taking the trails, bushwhacking, and crossing fences when needed to reach our destination.

I hiked down a grass path and over the rocky lakeshore and donned my swim cap, goggles, and shorter-for-mobility swimrun wetsuit in the post-storm rain. It was still raining heavily, as my dad and I entered the chilly water to swim across Toronto Lake to an island, with Parker in the kayak as our boat support.

Swimming in new open water is always unsettling. This lake, like most in Kansas, was sandy brown and I couldn't see much around me with my head underwater. The rain and waves blowing up in front of me added to the excitement of the day as I focused on swimming ahead to my destination after the long trail run before. About 200 yards from the island the storm picked back up and everything seemed to happen in a swirl. It started raining and blowing hard, raising whitecaps on the water, while a squall came in blinding our sighting. I pushed toward land and let Parker use the support boat to help navigate through the dangerous waters and wind.

Once on the deserted, swampy island I again felt like a native inhabitant of the land. I was cold and soaking wet, hiking around in the mud towing a swim buoy and boat around in the rainstorm. I felt like I was a Native American on a scouting adventure. The only difference was my fluorescent gear that created a striking contrast to the gray day around me.

We traipsed fast across the sinking primeval island, the kayak swaying behind us in the water littered with sticks that reached up to my knees. I was thankful for my wetsuit, as I didn't have to worry as much with that insulating layer on about becoming too cold and thankful for my swimrun shoes to protect my feet from the watery, rooty island swamp full of fallen timber. As strange as the uninhabited cross-island hike was, through a watery swamp, it was so much fun to be somewhere wild. We were battling the elements, in outlandish sport clothes get-ups no less, but out having fun in nature on what felt like a nautical exploration adventure on an island in the middle of a Kansas lake. The whole thing had a crazy, in-the-woods, expedition feel, which was invigorating and took my mind off the endurance challenge ahead.

After hiking to the other end of the island, it was time to wade back into the murky brown water, which was comforting and warm compared to the outside air at this point, and swim (kayak for Parker) across in another direction to a new section of the state park where my mom was waiting with our gravel bikes.

After exiting the second long swim portion, fueling and changing into bike gear, the sun came out just in time for the intense gravel biking portion of the 5 for 35 Multisport day. I knew from experience what clothes were best for running with a smooth transition into swimming and what worked best for biking after that, as I had practiced and planned my systems.

We traversed the Kansas Flint Hills for 15 intense up-and-down miles that ended in mudded trails leftover from the rain to connect with the next portion of the day: Kayaking on Fall River. Kansas biking is never easy, and these notorious hills, were as usual, full of wind, sun, and leg-demanding challenge. It was Parker's first real time on a biking adventure other than some rudimentary training. It was also his first time in the Flint Hills that rose and fell like small mountains around the prairie. With reoccurring prairie fires and cycles of drought through millennia, only the hardiest plants and animals adapted to survive life in the Flint Hills. It was beautiful, but evolutionary harsh. Parker started off fast and then learned the value of pacing oneself through the multisport experience the hard way. I am still not sure he has forgiven me for not giving him a better warning on what to expect. Like some things, multisport adventures are best experienced first-hand. No amount of explaining can detail what it is really like out on the open road, land and water.

After descending back down along the trees on the watershed, my mom met us waterside with the crew truck with our kayaks. The air cooled as we neared the rushing water, fully topped off from the day's earlier storms. We swapped the bikes for the boats and were ready for the flow. Under the cooler canopied trees strutting their greens, we were back on the water in time for more clouds, thunder and rain drops as we kayaked 10 miles down the Fall River to where it connected with the Fall River Lake Reservoir. We crossed the open lake to a cove where we set up for our final sport leg of stand up paddleboarding.

We pumped up our inflatable boards that had been stored in their packs in the crew truck and took to the water for the most relaxing portion of the day as we crossed the cove and back for the SUP portion and fifth multisport.

The 5 for 35 Multisport was a team effort with gear, transport, support, food, water and energy. We were up at 3 AM, naturally, and returned home about 10 PM with 12 hours of amazing adventure activities in between. I could not have celebrated so thoroughly without the help and sacrifice of my mom, dad, and Parker for helping make 5 for 35 happen. In this case, coordinating a child's birthday was not any easier for my parents after 35 years. It might have even been more demanding.

Holidays

In addition to birthdays, holidays make great days for multisport. Often, they include long weekends and extra time that begs to be filled with a life-affirming outdoor multisport adventure.

Labor Day SUP + Hike + Bike

One Labor Day, after I was newly married, my dad and I wanted to indoctrinate Parker fully into another multisport, now that he was officially part of the family. Enter the Labor Day SUP + Hike + Bike.

This long holiday weekend multisport combo had a new element from our usual holiday multisports, however. It was done in the evening, leading into night.

As the sun set, we pumped up our stand up paddleboards lakeside while the golden rays dipped down into orange sky set against the navy glass of the lake. We hopped on our boards and set off to skim the shore of the lake into the west watching the sun sink. As we reached our exit point of the suburban city lake, twilight faded in. We asked a friend who was a camp administrator to allow us use of the dock to exit and hike through a camp area with our SUP boards on our backs in their pack bags to the nearby country road. The only problem was the dock was coated in miry muck. Multisport is not a clean hobby. My hands and shoes were covered in the stinky mud, but that was all part of the fun.

We then trekked through the camp for a 1.5-mile uphill hike, the giant board packs reaching my knees and knocking into me while I walked. I liked the idea of hiking with the boards, but the reality was uncomfortable, muddy and smelly. However, I knew it was a short distance to where my mom met us with the crew truck to collect our SUP packs in exchange for our gravel bikes. By this point it was fully dark and the summer bugs paraded around us in the night, their clamor made louder by the stillness of the countryside. The stars shone above as we turned on our bike and helmet lights and flew down the old rails-to-trails bed downhill to home. We sped 17.5 miles back to the city, breaking giant cobwebs stretched out across the trail that lit up in the bike lights moments before crashing into them. They clung to our skin as our sweat soaked us, only noticeable when we stopped at road crossings and felt the cooling wind still.

We reached town and careened down a busy inner-city street past houses, factories, refineries, and midtown, speeding as fast as we could to escape the urban center and retreat to our river neighborhood. The county was soothing. The city was frightening. Especially on a Saturday night of a long holiday weekend. And on a bike.

This Labor Day SUP + Hike + Bike multisport combined it all: water, backpacking, country gravel biking, and urban exploring on a loud, hot summer night. All brought to us by multisport.

It was again an outdoor adventure . . . all within 20 miles of home.

New Year's Eve, New Year's Day & More Night Events

Night events enliven your multisport plans.

Growing up we used to compete in a New Year's Eve run that started downtown at midnight. Us neighborhood kids would gather in the convention center and try to make it to midnight, struggling to stay awake for the start of the race. The start gun would go off and we would be sent out into the night to run the city streets, sparkling under the stars on cold winter nights. It was daring for a child to see the city lit up in the middle of the darkening night. My dad always ran with us for safety while the other parents supported us by waiting for the after-run party and carting us home to bed.

We also kicked off cross country season at midnight on the official day that training was allowed. We ran downtown as well on those days thanks to the lights of the city.

Through the years I have always included night running, biking, swimming, paddling, climbing, and multisporting as an element to add in something extra and special.

Several birthdays included midnight runs and bikes though all ends of the city full of sweat and heat even in the dark. One of my dad's birthday events took place over 60k at night in the middle of December. Friends and family were invited to come overnight on the eve of his milestone 60th birthday and do what they could: run all, run a little, walk all, walk a little, or bike. This was its own version of multisport, with each person showing up in what way they could. Neighbors joined in for a short walk. Friends showed up for all or portions of the run. An uncle biked the dark sections of it with us. Homebase was my family home where all came and went between snacks and foam rolling, celebrating with whatever sport combo worked for us individually.

Many New Year's Days were spent for me running down trails, up and down old rails-to-trails that crossed the city, and along the Big Ditch end-to-end training for ultraruns and starting the new year with exercise and a hot tea to warm me up from the new January cold.

Chasing & Racing the Weather

One New Year's, not wanting to miss this fresh-start run I had become accustomed to, I took off for a run at 9 PM. The children were in bed and all I was missing was my downtime and sleep. An ice storm was coming, and I was racing to beat the storm. By changing my run time, I still had my outdoor workout and new year welcome. I could have waited until midnight or the morning, but it would have been too icy to run on the road. I wanted to make sure to get my outdoor workout in, especially to start off the fresh new year ahead.

We often raced the weather; saw it coming and worked to fit in an outdoor workout before a storm came. But we also chased the weather, often choosing to run, swim or kayak when the rain was called for so we could gain the added fun and challenge that comes with working out, training and multisporting outside in the untamed elements. When thinking about multisport, look for opportunities to both chase and race the weather. Since multisport is an all-weather, all-season activity, you don't have to be limited by the weather on any given day. Go out and see what happens by trying a new sport, sport progression, or new sport combination outside to enliven your training.

The multisport element of a New Year's run comes when you add a polar plunge swim. A polar plunge is a traditional way to welcome the new year by jumping in a cold body of water, going under, and swimming a short bit, to commemorate your craziness and the new season.

Run, bike, or hike to the water for even more racing excitement for a New Year's chasing thrill.

Interstates

Mixed Aquateering

When I first delved into the new multisport, I was inspired by mixed aquateering. Mixed aquateering came out of the Jackson Hole Picnic event involving biking to Jenny Lake in Grand Teton National Park, swimming across the cold lake in a wetsuit, hiking and then climbing using mountaineering techniques in the Tetons.

Bike/Ski

Bike Ski combos were also hot in the mountaineering world, with world-class skiers biking to their ski destinations in the mountains. The most intense renditions included climbing with a disassembled bike on one's back before skimoing back down for more biking. Bike ski combos were also used to cross long distances, traversing continents even, biking the trail portions and climbing and skiing through the mountainous ones.

Vol-Biv & Paralpinism

Vol-Biv is a paragliding combination of paragliding by air and hiking by foot to camp in between. Vol-Biv is adopted from French, meaning fly and bivouac. By flying and hiking to camp, paragliding adventurers can extend their outings to multiple days under their own power with all their gear on their backs. The mountain ranges of Europe are the most popular area for this combo as well as other alpine traverses.

Paralpinism is paragliding and climbing, or fly-to-climb. Participants use paragliding combined with climbing to reach previously inaccessible high peaks around the world. Like ski paragliding, the emergent combination of paralpinism creates new paths to remote mountains.

Mountain Challenges & FKTs

After reading about these combinations and other mountain triathlons, mountain climbing challenges—like the Nolan's 14 where the object was to climb as many 14ers, traveling on foot, in 60 hours—and fastest known time attempts on famous trails and wilderness routes that were being done at the time in and around the mountains, I was inspired to create more prairie events that would highlight the natural resources around me.

Run + Ride + Row: Raid to KanOkla

One of these such events was the Run + Ride + Row Raid to KanOkla that we dreamed up. My dad and another friend of ours put in weeks of planning, prepping, and training, woke up before 4 AM, covered 70 miles, and spent more than 13 hours running, biking, and kayaking to reach the Kansas and Oklahoma border.

My dad concepted the KanOkla event along the southern portion of the Arkansas River Water Trail, and Jeff and I decided it sounded like fun. This multisport adventure started with a 17-mile trail run along the river. We ran by the sandy banks from the center of town into the countryside, sheltered by thick trees and brush. We spotted eagles, owls, and deer along our path and

I assigned us each a spirit animal for the trek. The run began in the early dark and I loved traveling along the waterside path. With the raid's excitement buzzing inside, 17 miles felt quick and easy. It also felt effective. We covered the ground efficiently and went from our starting point to our fist transition relatively easily. Not all 17-mile runs are easy, so this felt like a special gift and a great way to be out exploring. By starting the raid with a run, the most physically demanding and high-impact portion of the day was over with and out of the way, much before the sun came up, so that mentally only having to bike and kayak felt more manageable for the remainder of the day.

I was thankful to have a solid base of running under my belt from my summer training along these river trails. Again, not all 17-mile runs conclude with 10 more hours of multisporting via biking and paddling, so I was glad to have committed to training for those events, too, leading up to the full raid taking place in the fall. Venturing farther afield to train in these new waters allowed me to learn more than the stretch of local river that fate had assigned.

At our first transition checkpoint, we hopped on our gravel bikes on country roads for about 15 miles to travel between river put ins. It felt nice to move from running to the easier biking, but as always, I was busy trying to keep pace with my dad and Jeff while on wheels.

Next up was a 10-mile kayak along the Arkansas River. My mom helped with shuttling the bike and boat gear between sections, so we met her at our fist river put in and loaded our bikes in the back of the crew truck after unloading the boats. Transitioning from lower body work from the running and biking to upper body work for the paddle was always a welcomed change. This was one of the best things about multisport. You were able to keep going, but rotate events along the way to stay excited and happily anticipating the next bend. By rotating events, segments, and sports, multisport allowed us to go farther and have more fun doing so.

Paddling this section of the Arkansas River south of town was enjoyable as the banks towered high above, much taller than the in-town shore. I paddled along the narrow brown water splattered with sandbars, enthralled with the sandy banks on each side closing in on me around my usually wide-open river. Giant tree roots exposed from the ever constant rising and lowering of water and the effects of erosion offered some sort of metaphor on life that I could never quite put the right words to. It was something about change and meaning, putting down roots and having them torn back up, adapting, rebuilding, and floating on downstream, no matter the storm. The message changed each time I paddled the section, evolving with me.

For the immediate, the new put in and access areas offered different local maps to study and areas to chart. Names like Rainbow Bend and Gouda Springs lent history to go along with the trail. Gouda Springs was named after local salt springs that had been there since the area was settled. Walnut Park, Chestnut Street, and Pecan Grove's names echoed areas of dense trees where past generations of my family had picked and harvested nuts, I learned on the raid.

Exploring a new section of waterway brought a discovery element to the raid that made it about more than simply an endurance feat. We were traveling through our own lands via human power. We were crossing state lines by our own propulsion. We were going to Oklahoma by running there, biking there, and kayaking there. I had run this way on backroads prior and completed some sections of the kayak for training bouts, but I hadn't combined all three for a multisport before. The idea of kayaking to the next state was even more exciting for its uniqueness, all packaged by multisport.

This sunny daytime paddle was followed by another bike leg, another kayak leg, and then a final bike leg, a little more than 10 miles each.

I started feeling tired on each but used the momentum of an anticipated change to keep moving forward in my quest. I was also thrilled to be traveling more in another direction on the newly named water trail. The National Water Trails System is a network of water trails open to the public and a subset of the National Recreation Trails Program that provides close-to-home recreation opportunities. By being out on a new National Water Trail, I was exploring, learning, and studying one of America's rivers. The more time I spent on the rivers and trails, the more I wanted to protect and restore them as well, on clean ups and volunteering with community groups. We created a multisport that allowed us to celebrate this new trail while recreating and appreciating the valuable shorelines along the way.

After powering through the final bike leg, we finished at the Kansas Oklahoma state line right at the sunset golden hour. We celebrated with snacks from the truck and shared some with our new furry adventure friend, a kind dog who welcomed our team at the border. We ordered takeout pizza from our favorite place in town the night before and packed it to have in the cooler after our raid, following the systems guideline to have fuel in place post-event. We knew that having a good solid refueling plan for our dinner would be a little motivation at the end and provide recovery nutrition in the middle of nowhere when we couldn't easily buy something. Even the gas stations along the highway were a long way off.

This multisport day wasn't a race, but it was very much based in the test of endurance, covering three disciplines of running, riding, and rowing, with many miles and hours of emotions, hunger and fatigue included. The suffering was all worth it to run, bike and row to another state! It was a day full of challenge and human-generated exploration as we followed a new trail in a creative combination.

Another watery multisport day that comes to mind when talking about interstates is from a family trip to Branson, Missouri. My entire family met up to support my cousin in one of her performances in the Ozark vacation town. On the weekend we rented a boat to take on Table Rock Lake, with my grandmother in tow. It seemed rather tame, so that morning, my dad and I found a local 5k run to compete in. We woke up early, ran the race, ended up soaked in humid sweat, and made it back before anyone else was up. Later that day, my dad found the point in the lake between the states of Missouri and Arkansas. Then my cousin and I jumped off the boat and swam across the state line between Missouri and Arkansas. These two daily life activities were a way to infuse multisport concepts into a family vacation, giving it our own adventure style as we challenged ourselves, explored interstates and had more fun.

Linkages

Multisport gives you the ability to link sports and natural elements together.

These linkages can take the form of linking rivers together with a custom trail, or lakes with a charted path. In Patagonia, I linked two countries together, those of Argentina and Chile, on a multiday adventure run race through the volcanic region. Linkages can include linking mountains by running or biking between them to push the limits of endurance, climbing and sport combinations. In the other direction, down, linkages can also include slot canyons. My dad stashed a bike on a trip and after hiking through slot canyons and gulches in the American Southwest, he then rode his bike uphill back to his original trailhead. This combination of sport and geological destination allows you to do more than simply rappel a wall or hike a mountain. It allows you to go farther physically, mentally, emotionally, and spiritually as you generate ideas and ways to multisport.

On a hot run and need to cool off? Hop in your local lake that you are running by. You can plan your route to include highlights like these, or you can be spontaneous. Use the multisport mindset to see new ways to explore and chase them down. I had no plans to jump in the fishing lake at Sedgwick County Park that day on a hot run home. However, after a running buddy jumped in, I couldn't resist. I was invigorated by tapping into the multisport spirit of seizing an opportunity to get wet, try something new, and dream up linkages.

The Packing Combinations

Packrafting (Run/Raft/Run)

When I learned about packrafts, the inflatable rafts that you could inflate, deflate, and wear on your back in between, I jumped into packrafting multisport adventures using my neighborhood rivers. This new sport combination came to me during a difficult time in my life, and it gave me a new challenge to learn, a new way to explore, and new fun to find.

For a run/paddle workout, I started with a two-mile run to my water put-in on the Big Arkansas River, with the packraft on my back in my bigger running backpack that I used to run across the desert of Namibia and America's Grand Canyon Rim 2 Rim 2 Rim. Upon arriving at my entry point, I then aired up the kayak-like raft and set off for six miles of paddling down the river to the last exit before the dam. Then I deflated the raft and packed it back up on my back for a four-mile run home.

It was wonderful to run and paddle while being totally self-sufficient with all my gear on my back. I liked feeling fully supported and able to go as far as needed by my own power.

Bikerafting (Bike/Raft/Bike)

Next, I tried my new packraft with a bike/packraft/bike combo.

I rode 10 miles northwest of town on my gravel bike with the packraft packed on my back. After arriving at my water put-in, I found a flat spot under a bridge to air up the boat and disassemble the bike to attach it up front on the packraft, with a little help from my dad. We then set off on a paddle down the Arkansas River, my second home and watery friend. We covered about five miles as we paddled downstream.

Once we reached our river exit, we deflated the boats, packed them, reassembled the bikes, and biked five miles home for a cold and wet adventure all close to urban comforts, but still very much out in the wilds. (There were hunters on our route that we had to navigate around to avoid being shot at. It is Kansas after all.)

This form of sport is also called bikerafting. I like it because you can combine the two to go on extreme trips in remote places or around your own region. The leaders in the sport combine fat bikes and packrafts for long trips over rugged terrain and mountain ranges, inventing new linkages of sports and routes. The packraft solves the exploration problem of crossing bodies of water.

This idea of packing travel combinations gives multisport more ways to cover longer distances.

Backpacking & Fastpacking

Backpacking is hiking with packs, good for long trips and including family and friends at any age. Fastpacking is a trimmed down version of this with minimal pack gear and a speedy pace, like I had done crossing the Grand Canyon's gorges and back again. It is a mix between heavy hiking, backpacking, trekking, walking, and running.

Bike, Scooter & SUPpacking

Bikepacking and biketouring allow you to load gear on your bike for packing, touring, and camping over trails, paths, and even for some, across continents. I had plans to take the children in the chariot bike towing stroller on family bikepacking trips.

SUPpacking, SUP touring, SUP camping and expedition SUP are also new options. These encompass multiple-day camping trips on paddleboards and expedition-like crossings, even reaching to ultra-distance SUP events. Since I always ended up wet, I knew quality dry bags would be important for any overnight SUP journeys of my own.

Another option here is foot-bike packing, or scooter packrafting, where scooters are ridden in place of bikes for long-distance packing and packrafting trips on wheels.

Rafting & Swimpacking

Rafting camping trips and expeditions down rivers have been around for years, and I had some planned for my family with our new whitewater raft in addition to some raft multi-sport combos.

A new kind of individual rafting journey is swimpacking, also known as cross country swimming and swim hiking. Swim-packing is an emergent sport that I had just amassed the gear for, floating your dry bag atop an inflatable tow buoy that enabled you to swim across lakes and other bodies of water and camp in between with your dry gear.

Parker and I tried it one spring morning. Squeezing our-selves into our triathlon wetsuits, we organized our gear on the beach of a swimming lake. We packed our dry bags full of phones, car keys, swim bags, towels, and a special picnic pouch to enjoy upon crossing the lake. Since it was spring, the water was still cool, and we wanted to practice in our wetsuits to maxi-mize this type of packing's potential for the most all-weather, close to year-round (April-October open-water swimming season in the Midwest) fun. Pulling the raft behind me with it tethered around my waist was easy as I was used to pulling a swim buoy for visibility when crossing an open body of water. I quickly forgot about all the valuables atop the raft and swam like normal having an enjoyable time in the water. After the crossing, we pulled out our perfectly dry picnic and hiked to our next destination, stowing the wetsuits and donning shoes. For more, we could have kept swimming and traveling on a swim hiking route to end in an overnight campout if desired. It once again felt great to throw all my gear on a raft and tow it while open-water swimming, having everything needed to get up and get out. Cross country swimming offered another way to create multisport adventures on land and water, crossing both while doing so.

Skirafting

For November-March in the Midwest, skirafting combines the mobility of packrafts in cold climes where land is crossed and climbed via skis with the packrafts strapped on and pulled behind over the terrain between bodies of water, like an arctic pulk sled harness, or like we did when we skied or snowshoed with our stroller's convertible wheels-to-skis attachment. In the winter, I could skiraft or snowshoeraft across my street to my river and packraft down it, similar to the skirafting sport leaders who explored icefields and glacial polar regions by skiraft.

Roller Versions

Rollerboating, where you inline skate with the packraft on your back in between water sections is an option to do or integrate here as well, for a full-on multisport mix up. Skip the boat and go for bladepacking or ultrablading for long-distance inline skating challenges. When you add the backpack for bladepacking, you gain the self-sufficiency element and can cover long distances unsupported, just like bikepacking, or scooterpacking, but on smaller wheels.

The packing options can also be done on shorter trips or midweek overnights.

We could packraft with bikes and bivy camp overnight in the wilderness and sandbar areas right in the middle or our town, or not too far from it. We could swimpack and seek out wilderness and new multisport expedition ideas linking bodies of local water. These mini adventures were full of new challenge, but it motivated us to do deep local exploring in search of new areas to bike, paddle, swim, campout and more.

These new combos were full of inspiration. I liked the new self-supported endeavors because they gave the individual user control and agency for creating their own adventures wherever they were using the natural elements around them, exactly what I liked to do.

Packrafting, bikerafting, backpacking, fastpacking, bikepacking, SUPpacking, scooter packrafting, rafting expeditions, swimpacking, skirafting, snowshoerafting, rollerboating and bladepacking are packing combinations that add fun, challenge, and exploration to your world via the idea of multiple sports combined into one multisport outing, event, expedition, crossing, tour, camp and or ultra.

Three Pack: Swim Tow/Gravel Bikeraft/Packraft

Wanting to integrate more of the packing combos into our multisport lifestyle, Parker and I planned a three packing version swim/bike/paddle multisport for the fall with a swim across Cheney Lake with the packrafts towed behind us, bikes strapped atop, followed by a bike from the lake on country back roads with the packrafts attached to our backs while on our bikes, to the Arkansas River that we would bikeraft down back to home, the bikes strapped to the front of the rafts.

The genesis for this smaller trip idea started with wanting to find an adventure close to home that wouldn't take us too far away from Penelope and Lachlan and that included swimming for me and more packrafting for Parker who had recently invested in one and was looking for more opportunities to use it.

For swimming, we knew we would start at our closest lake. From there, since I had already swum across this lake at its farthest point, we looked for an out-of-the way area in the narrow section to the west (to avoid boat and other motorized traffic) that would be a good crossing spot. We then reconnoitered the spot and did a test swim and paddle across it in the summer. The new challenge would be completing the swim while towing the packrafts with bikes on them and pulling them swim buoy-style across the water on what could be a windy, foggy, or cold (wetsuits required) morning. Another reason for swimming across the western section was that we wanted to reach the Arkansas River for packrafting. This western crossing spot on the lake allowed us to spend the least distance gravel biking down backcountry roads (that we also test drove on our info gathering trip) to the river put-in spot. Along the Arkansas River we would paddle downstream with the bikes on our packrafts into town and toward home. After a portage, we could paddle to the river section nearby and exit right at our house. The Three Pack was another living example of deep exploring close to home.

We used a road atlas and gazetteer with a detailed topographical map to plot our course and confirmed it with on-the-ground scouting and online mapping tools. Multisport events always began with an idea and a solid, researched plan.

Through the years, I swam this area, biked through it, and paddled down it, but I had not yet linked it together in this way. With multisport, I was able to take a local area that was known in an individual way, and create something new by combining routes, linkages, waterways and sports.

Now that we knew what we were doing and where we were doing it, we needed to work on the how. The first step here was to make sure we had the right gear and knew how to use it.

Swim Gear

Open-water swim cap (bright color)

Open-water swim googles (wider for more peripheral vision and tinted to see in the sun)

Swim costume (since the swim here is followed by a bike, this for me is my triathlon suit top and bottoms, rather than just a swimsuit for maximized bike comfort)

Tech socks (want a fast-drying option)

Swimrun shoes (all-weather shoes that I can swim in and then wear for biking and packrafting)

Wetsuit (if water is below 75 degrees Fahrenheit on Three Pack multisport day)

Bike Gear

Gravel bike (transported in packraft)

Helmet (transported in backpack in packraft)

Biking glasses with strap for paddling (transported in backpack in packraft)

Biking gloves (transported in backpack in packraft)

Go Far book personalized Buff (transported in backpack in packraft)

Bike fixing & repair tools (on frame)

Extra repair kits for all gear (in transition area or support vehicle)

Packraft Gear

Backpack to hold packraft, inflator, paddle & personal items

Packraft with tow line & belt

Packraft inflator

Packraft paddle
PFD
Paddling hat

Personal Items in Backpack

Phone in waterproof case
Map in waterproof case
Hydration bladder
    with water
Food for multi-hour
    caloric needs
Electrolytes in water bottle
Lip balm
Sunscreen
Bug spray
Advil
Extra hair tie & bobby pins
Knife
Water whistle
Vaseline for areas that might
    rub when wet
Packraft patch kit
Emergency matches
Emergency blanket
Bivy sack
Headlamp
Extra batteries
Signaling mirror
Tow rope
Bail bucket & sponge
First aid kit
Boat lights
Duct tape
Emergency female supplies
Toilet paper kit with wet
    wipes, hand sanitizer,
    and disposal plan
    (trowel/pack out bags/
    use leaves)
Safety pins (have had these
    in my event bag since old
    racing bib number days)
Carabiners
Bungee cords
Rain gear
Warm layers in event
    of capsize
Warm gloves
Warm hat
Handwarmers
Walkie-Talkies

Money (cash & card)
ID
GPS tracker & charger in
    waterproof case

Phone charging bank in
    waterproof case
Extra food
Extra water

Each of these systems had to be tested and practiced before event day. We mapped our personal gear, equipment, food and hydration, safety, communication, route finding, and backups for everything. We tested towing the packrafts and most importantly, disassembling and assembling our gravel bikes and how to best attach them to the packrafts with their front and back tires stacked on top of the bow, as well as the most effective way to inflate and deflate the boat. We decided against the extra step of disassembling the bikes, like we did in the early days of packrafting, instead, strapping the bikes across the boats. We chose to pack our boats in backpacks on our backs while biking, but another option included attaching the deflated boats to the bike handles, if more gear was needed for the backpack.

We would also need crew. My dad volunteered to drop us at the lake for our crossing, kayak with us, and haul our gear in the back of his truck. He would also meet us along the way for safety and to give us more water and fuel as needed so we didn't have to tow our bike with as much as we would need on a 15 plus-mile packraft downriver. We planned the Three Pack to be self-supported, and it could be that, however knowing we had a teammate along in case of an emergency was the safest option, especially as new parents.

Three Pack Training

I trained for this fall event in the summer months of June, July and August. I had recently come off a 100-mile ultrapaddle expedition, so the paddling portion was not a concern, as I was in good shape for that leg. I made a goal of getting on the water a couple of times each month, even if it was in the form of stand up paddleboarding, to keep my paddle muscles flowing and fluid.

My main base training was running. I knew if I could keep my endurance up with weekly 6, 10, or 12-mile runs, I could be ready for almost any endurance event at any time. My years of multisport training taught me this. Running allowed me to maintain a solid, year-round base to use as a jumping off point for other sports or more in-depth specification training.

I always loved open-water swimming, especially in the summer, so I set a goal of a couple of swims a week. One could be in the pool for efficiency's sake, but the other should be in open-water to best enjoy one of my treasured summer activities of submerging myself in a crisp blue-green lake and swimming across it. This was an example of a fun goal. The Three Pack event gave me a reason to commit to getting as much summer swimming in as possible to enjoy the season and train for a future multisport event ahead.

I spent the years post-college still training like a triathlete or a distance swimmer. I focused mainly on swimming freestyle and going for distance. Since coming back to the water after having my children, I changed my swimming and started incorporating back more of the other strokes, drills, intervals, and swim training tools. I no longer wanted to only be a long-distance freestyler. I wanted to work each of my muscles in as many ways as possible to regain strength and fitness and continue to challenge myself. I wanted to feel the speed of more intervals and tap into new cardiovascular peaks by swimming fast and activating my fast-twitch muscles. Rather than going back to swimming like an age grouper or Masters swimmer, I added these training techniques with my marathon, open-water, distance swimming skills to be the most well-versed swimmer I could be. I was using multisport in the form of different ways, styles, and strokes of swimming and it rounded out my swimming experience.

As a young parent, I wondered if I would ever go on a long bike ride alone again. My outside rides were short and focused on destinations, often with a stroller pulled along behind me. The added weight of a child or children made for great cross-training, but I did miss my time on the open road. Long bike rides were for another time in my life. I completed short indoor sessions weekly, always wanting to keep my body used to time in the saddle, and I planned to rely on my other cardio training and years of muscle memory to complete the gravel bike section of the Three Pack. I would like to say that this type of bike commitment was an anomaly to new parenting, but biking had always been my weakest link, and I often felt I should be training more on the bike. But I found by focusing on what I enjoyed most, I was a happier athlete all around.

I also used strength and mobility training to prepare for The Three Pack.

Weightlifting makes me feel strong and helps me perform better. I like mobility training as well as it integrates functional fitness moves that translate into real life. Mobility training uses bodyweight or light to medium weights and exercises that are easy to do without complicated equipment. Both traditional weightlifting with compound moves that net strength gains and mobility training with its focus on function are important when aiming to achieve peak fitness for multisport.

When I swam competitively growing up, I dreaded dryland strength training. It always felt uncomfortable. Kind of like running, bodyweight and weight work is uncomfortable, because you are challenging yourself, offering your body something new to overcome, and it in turn must adapt.

My senior year in high school, I took a weights class as an elective. It would teach me all the traditional weightlifting moves and I hoped, improve my running and swimming. It was the best decision and a great learning ground.

I was thankful for my base knowledge and experience from this the next summer as I trained on my own at my local gym before heading off to row on the Kansas State Crew Team. As a Division I collegiate athlete, we had dedicated weight training as part of our workouts. We had devoted team strength and conditioning coaches, and it was intense. I learned Olympic lifts and powerlifting. There was so much competition to lift more every day. Not being a fast-twitch-muscle athlete and being one of the smaller athletes on the team, this was a constant challenge for me, but I pushed myself to lift more and more and squat and bench my weight and above, competing daily on the water and in the weight room.

After my rowing experience, I started lifting on my own at the gym, working different muscle groups each day, striving for maximum weight with low to medium sets, in the bodybuilding fashion that I was drawn to at the time. I carried this way of strength training with me through those college years to set off my triathlon and adventure racing.

Post college, I kept the traditional heavy lifts, but always liked the group fitness classes I did on the weekends where I worked every body part in a one-hour class with more of a muscular endurance focus. This was efficient, effective, and worked best for my body. I was never a powerlifter or able to consistently perform super heavy lifts. Heavy weights and pull-ups eluded me, but I found a different kind of strength. It was the strength of endurance; the strength to keep going. Rather than fight against my body, I trained with it using the body self-awareness I gained as an endurance athlete. I still made sure to throw in new resistances to keep from being too comfortable, but I learned being strong manifested in a multitude of ways, not only the traditional ones. As a slow-twitch, endurance athlete, this worked best for me. I was also certified to teach group fitness classes, and liked the choreography aspect that was interesting, changed up moves, and challenged me in new spatial ways. I carried this style of lifting through my endurance racing and multisporting around the world.

Recently, I added my steel mace, steel clubs, bag, and ad hoc tools from martial arts disciplines that give me weights and mobility in one, an overall trend in fitness. Movement training for me also includes bodywork practices like yoga, Pilates, barre, and any and all myofascial work.

What I found works best to complement the Three Pack and other multisport endurance sports training is this type of movement strength training:

One day a week of traditional strength training:

Working all muscles in an hour, lifting at a medium rate, but pushing to lift heavier when appropriate. I like to do this in a group fitness class.

One day a week of mobility-style training:

Using total body fitness moves with lots of choreography to keep dialed in. I like to do this in a group fitness class.

One day a week of bodywork:

Including yoga, Pilates, barre, and myofascial work done in a group fitness class, private class or alone.

This combination makes strength training a successful and integral part of my fitness base as a multisport athlete. In between these strength days I include cardio days, which are my key sports of swimming, biking, running and paddling. With this mix, I am always ready to test a new form of cross training or a new self-propelled sport for all around multisport and multiuse training based on body self-awareness.

With the right, tested systems, and the right training, I was ready to take on my next multisport, The Three Pack, a swim/bike/paddle packing combo of swimming while towing a packraft with a bike attached to it, gravel bikerafting with the packraft on my back in a backpack, and packrafting with my bike strapped to the boat while wearing my backpack as I paddled.

Three Pack Event Day

When this Three Pack multisport day arrived, the planned open-water lake swim tow/gravel bikeraft/packraft, turned into a packraft tow and river trek once we reached the drought stricken Arkansas River.

By being immersed in the waters and lands of Kansas, we saw first-hand the effects of the severe Midwest drought that fall with low water levels evident in reservoirs, rivers, streams, and creeks along our route.

The lake waters receded with more wading than ever before needed to reach our swim starting point. We donned wetsuits and strapped our packrafts to our waists with our tow lines. The water was cool and startling, but it was fun to pull all my gear, my boat, and my bike behind me in the water. I had everything I needed and could go anywhere, as long as I could keep swimming!

On the biking portion, once reaching dry land again and packing our gear to be contained on the bike ride, we noticed how low the streams and creek beds were, with most being completely empty.

Once we reached the river, disembarking our gravel bikes and inflating our boats, we realized that paddling would be nearly impossible.

We hiked down, balancing a boat in one hand, a paddle in the other, and gave it our best go, as we jumped in the rafts and took off downstream.

The next several hours consisted of springing in and out of the boats with packs and paddles, trying desperately to catch the current, to not much avail. After exhausting ourselves expending loads of energy on this, I decided to commit to walking the river.

As we trekked the river bends with the packrafts attached to our waists with the tow lines, I thought, how fortuitous. When we began planning this event, we did not know we would need tow lines to walk the Arkansas River. After monitoring the weather and landscape conditions, we decided that the possibility of needing to walk the river, pulling a boat behind, would be just as important as paddling the river, if only to bring awareness to the low water levels.

Our pace was slow. Paddling a river can be tedious if there are a lot of twists and turns. Walking, or sloshing through shallow water, sand and mid-stream island navigation was glacial.

However, I loved being in the wilderness. In my river. I loved knowing that there was no way out, only through. We were the only humans for miles, certainly the only ones in a river with scarcely any water in it, and we had no access to the outside world until at least the next bridge.

I was in the water, walking another river. It was once again a new way to feel it, see it, discover it and experience it. By walking the river's sandy bottom, I was able to connect with it and my land even more. There was nowhere else I needed to be, but walking the river, towing a boat, to home.

These new packing combinations offer even more possibilities for homegrown multisport adventures, linkages, interstates, and rivers.

Running Rivers & River Running

I paddled up and down my rivers in dozens of watercrafts and millions of ways. These were not the obvious choices for recreation in town. The water was brown, although I was excited on days when I could spy a green tint glinting off the surface. While the Big Arkansas and Little Arkansas Rivers flowed through Wichita, activity centered around their joining point in the downtown corridor. For years the rivers were neglected as an entertainment opportunity as modern life led people more indoors and less out. More recently, the twin river's power and draw has been attempted to be harnessed with more people taking to the water in recreational kayaks and SUPs.

However, with runoff waters from outskirting farms and city streets, the water of my rivers was known as not being safe to eat or drink from or use on high effluviant days. Farmland fertilizers, pesticides, and manure could often be found in high amounts, like the pollution in other prairie rivers. That had never kept me out. I simply tried not to get my head wet or go under, even if that was bound to happen every now and then when boating on the water. Being a central part of my life, I decided to embrace the vagary of the rivers and play in them anyway. Life was too short to avoid the water.

The Five Confluences

I wanted to run the rivers and river run so much that I created five distinct points to do so using watershed confluences, despite it not being a popular choice for outdoor fun. I simply created my own. I knew adventure was out there. I just had to go out and find it. Multisport might not always be your easy choice. But it will let you experience the wonder and inspire you to go. Running Rivers and River Running for multisport was the opposite of limiting. It was in all ways expanding and expansive.

I linked the Big Arkansas River and the Big Ditch canal system to the North and South with runs to each and a paddle too at the North on my 34th birthday. I linked the Big Arkansas River and Little Arkansas Rivers at their North meeting point by running to it and paddling back down on my Birthday 33 Multisport day. The fourth piece of the puzzle was the historic meeting of the Big and Little Rivers at the center of town at their South confluence. This sacred spot between the two rivers was in the middle of my city in downtown Wichita. In more recent years it served as a focal point and tourist attraction along the river and featured the Keeper of the Plains statue, a symbol of the confluence and emblem of our city.

This area was also noted by several historic markers, signaling the life moving along the river though time, distance, and change. In the 1860s and 1870s cowboys moved cattle from Texas along the Chisholm Trail, crossing the Arkansas River to the stockyards and railheads. By running these rivers, I was running through history.

One early summer morning, as the sun rose among the hazy heat of August, I ran across the slopping dam where the two rivers met, carefully balancing on the slimy narrow concrete, fast to cross to the looming Keeper statue before light dawned. As I dodged rafts of ducks and gaggles of familiar geese, I felt the refreshing waters of both Arkansas Rivers rush over my feet, hot from running, as I navigated between my two rivers. What a moment to join them together by human power, although I had to push that moment to make sure I was not caught in the bold act of running on top of a flowing dam in the humid mist.

After that crossing by foot, another human-powered adventure begged to be undertaken that combined kayaking and portaging the boats via land. I had not yet connected the two rivers at one go on one paddling day at their confluence point. On a summer afternoon, just off maternity release from having my daughter, Parker, my dad, and I took off paddling in our blue, red, and green kayaks from home on the Little River. We paddled to the confluence point of the Little and Big Arkansas Rivers then exited our boats, bushwhacked up the bank while hauling kayaks, portaged the kayaks across several streets and a parking lot to avoid the large dangerous upper dam region, bushwhacked the bank back down with the kayaks, and put the boats back in on the Big Arkansas River. We added more daring to a normal river paddle while adding more meaning by linking these rivers by our own engine power of paddling and portaging.

It was empowering to once again be out adventuring, carrying a kayak on my shoulder, weighed down by its heaviness, clamoring up banks, and crossing busy streets. It made me feel connected to myself and the outside world again, as well as the men and women of the prairie who had come before me, having children, fording, and portaging over the Plains, in different ways, but similar all the same. After the painful, as they all are carrying a heavy kayak, but meaningful portage back down the Big Arkansas River, we flowed on to more adventures downstream.

One of those adventures was adding a third section to this watershed triad of linkages with a fifth confluence point. On a wet spring training day, I linked where the Big Arkansas and the city's drainage canal on Interstate 35 flow together through the middle of town.

I was training for canyoneering at the time, so hiking through ankle-deep, cold water on a windy, wet spring day was fitting. However, hiking down the inner-city canal with highways bisecting above felt rogue and wild in an opposite way from exploring in the backcountry. To exit the canal, I had to crawl through a box culvert at a secret, abandoned destination followed by jumping over a fence and rolling under a passageway. This was a classic multisport urbex experience.

These multisport examples linked the rivers and waterways around me, involving running, kayaking, packrafting, bikepacking, biking, swimming, and more. The challenges came in the forms of portaging and paddling, and the exploration came in the form of linking the routes together. The fun was all around us. It can be all around you too when you apply these tenets of multisport and come up with your own.

6 | Learning From My Multisport Experience

Get Fluid

My first tenet of multisport is, "Water Is Life." And I am talking about more than just proper hydration. I am drawn to the water, especially on hot summer days (and on warm, cool, and cold ones, too!) That is why, when I am building a new multisport event, I will usually start around water.

This water can take the form of a pool, lake, river and/or a swim, raft, frozen crossing or more. When it comes to creating your multisport and your own foundational tenets, you can start with what you have near you. Look for opportunities to integrate multisport and take advantage of the new things you have around you when you travel for work, vacation, and expedition, as well.

The Four Lake Weekend: Swimrunning, Kayaking & Running

One of my favorite ways to celebrate water and use the water I had near me was on a weekend I called the Four Lake Weekend.

On this weekend, my family and I multisported to four area lakes over a few short days.

The Four Lake Weekend started with the goal of getting in as much water as possible, which is always an objective of mine, especially during a sweltering Kansas summer.

On Saturday morning, I ran and swam on part of my swimrun route that took me through three lakes, plus a few other waterways and swamps that I added to explore, like the city's Big Ditch floodway, our two rivers that wind in and out of town, and some explorative wild swimming in area ponds. While the rivers and lakes were clean enough, the ponds and swampy areas were too stagnant and runoff-based for me to add them into permanent route rotation. That was the explorative side of multisport, begging me to try something new, seek out a novel water feature, swim it, explore it, and then either love it or decide it was not ideal.

On Sunday, my mom, dad, Parker, and I headed to a fourth lake east of town for discovery paddling. I had previously swum across this lake while six weeks pregnant with my daughter on a rainy cloudy day. I swam the lake west of town the previous year, and by crossing both by my own propulsion, those crossings allowed me to claim my place between the two. At El Dorado Lake this weekend, we then paddled our kayaks through the long lake fingers, investigating each section, something that I had always wanted to do. I camped, boated, sailed, and swam at this lake, but exploring the tiny backend parts of it in a kayak was a new element I was happy to add.

Thus, we capped off a Four Lake Weekend. On our way home near the dam, Parker and I sprinted as fast as we could up to the top, to add one more multisport element of fun.

This ever-classic run/swim combo is one of my ultimate go-to multisports because running and swimming are the most effective, efficient, and lively endurance sports for me. I like to do them together whenever possible, even if it is only running to the downtown YMCA for a swim or running to my open-water lake spot. My *Water Is Life* motto motivates me to include a run/swim combo whenever possible.

Water Board: Swim/SUP/Yoga/Proneboard

One weekend, Parker and I participated in a SUP yoga class at an area lake with our yoga studio. We stepped up this activity and turned it into a multisport by attaching the SUP ankle straps to our feet and swimming our boards out, then paddling to the yoga spot, where we anchored the boards and did a yoga session on top of the boards with the class. On our way to the beach start area, we proneboarded them back, lying face down, prone, on our boards and swimming with our arms. I was encouraged knowing that people did this for endurance-level miles as part of ocean racing, like from the Hawaiian island of Molokai to the Hawaiian island of Oahu for 32 miles across the Ka'iwi Channel. Our Swim/SUP/Yoga/Prone Water Board started with what we were already doing and added new and different sport combinations to make it multiport at a reasonable, local level.

Integrating proneboarding and learning about its role in distance racing around the world and in the Pacific motivated me to do it more often and use it in my multisport round up. It was like swimming on a paddleboard to me, and I liked it, just as I had liked what I called swimboating where I used my arms as paddles in my whitewater kayak at training camp.

SUP Triathlon & SUP 6+

One summer weekend, Parker and I had a chance to escape for the day to our local westerly lake where we created a SUP Triathlon multisport. The three SUP-based sports coincided with our third wedding anniversary. I always seek out these types of playoffs, especially with multisports.

First, we swam across our lake, at a researched and appropriate spot, while towing our stand up paddleboards. We arrived at a private beach for this outdoor day date and hiked up and down enjoying the calm, peace and vegetation lakeside. Then we paddled on top of the boards back until we arrived at the last section where we laid face down on the boards and paddled with our arms for my new favorite proneboarding.

We could have stuck with SUP only, but by adding multisport components, we had more fun, changed up our sporting routine, worked more muscles, and had an overall more well-rounded day of outside athletics with challenge and exploring as well.

We bought cookies and iced tea on the way home to further celebrate and refuel for an evening ahead with the children. We had to maximize our time and multisport allowed us to do just that.

To take the SUP Triathlon and expand it to the SUP Six, we next plan to trek with the boards on our backs for one, stand up paddleboard for two, swim while towing the board for three, anchor and do yoga on top of the board for four, prone board for five, to a wavy section of the lake and SUP surf for six ways to multisport SUP all in one day on one body of water at one time. This sports combo gives us such a huge efficiency of bringing together efforts and sports. An example of when you are pressed for time, maxing out on different ways to SUP in one day is a new-parent-must.

Throw in TRX bands attached to an area tree branch on the SUP for a seventh option, now making the SUP Seven possible. With more ideas and varieties, come more add-ons and ways to expand your multisport days.

SUP/Strength/Swim

Another time, I paddled on a SUP for yoga at a private lake then participated in a beach CrossFit workout with bodyweight exercises on the land interspersed with swim sprints in the water. I loved the combination of sports as well as the combination of systems it worked: Endurance for the paddling and high-intensity intervals for the bodywork and fast swimming.

Obstacle Challenges & Swim Obstacles

Obstacle challenges are a key component of adventure racing, which means they *can* be a key component of multisport. Obstacle runs and mud runs are easy ways to become involved in adventure racing and try the multisport concept.

One of the first true mud run events that I competed in was an adventure race that involved trail running and mountain biking with obstacle and mud challenges in between. My team alternated with the same bike, at some points carrying it overhead through lakeside water crossings, while one person ran and one person rode, relay-style. The bike was decorated with streamers to help us locate our own in the crowded transitions organized by race numbers. The final portion of this mud run was the mud pit where we had to belly crawl under ropes covered from head-to toe-in the sticky slop that nearly reached my eyes.

Another of my favorite obstacle adventure races was a five-hour event through the red clay dirt of Georgia in the American South. My dad and I talked my best friend into joining us on this race to make a three-person mixed gender team. Melinda was my friend from competitive swimming, so she was no stranger to the fitness adventure racing required. This event combined mountain biking on beautiful, wooded trails, inflatable kayaking on what looked like a placid lake surrounded by green trees, until paddling it in full sun, trail running, and even a swim.

Melinda and I were thrilled about the swim portion where we crossed one side of a lake to another during a running leg. The biking and kayaking, however, were totally out of her comfort zone, so we worked together to solve each section and make our way through the viny, mossy undergrowth.

After five hours of intense racing, in our matching light blue team racing jerseys, we reached the obstacle section at the very end of the race. A race of this duration was a muddled middle ground at not quite a sprint pace but also short enough to not be in full long-distance mode. We were stuck sprinting for speed, but also pacing ourselves to make it through for a full five hours of non-stop endurance.

At the very end of this hurdle, we faced the final obstacle challenges. We had to jump hay bales, pull ourselves over high bars, swing through the middle triangle of a plywood structure, climb cargo nets, and then scale a huge wall by hauling ourselves up a rope one at a time. Muscles tensed, tired, and shaking, we worked as a team as each of us pushed to the very end, mounting the wall and sprinting to the finish, sweaty and dirty from the red mud. Our efforts earned us a spot on the Balance Bar racing website as we gritted up the final wall.

Water obstacle courses exist and could make for an enticing destination multisport, ending with one of these set ups. Swim obstacle races are also an idea. For these, I am inspired by the Neptune Steps event. This event takes place swimming in cold water in a canal in the UK. You swim upstream against the current passing obstacles in the form of ladders, ropes, and cargo nets at each of the locks, climbing them mid-swim. Training includes swim training, cold water training and obstacle training. From childhood days running homemade obstacle courses in my backyard, to scaling walls and climbing rope nets during adventure races in the U.S., obstacles are a constant in the multisport lifestyle.

All obstacle races take endurance, strength, and agility training, making them standout multisport endeavors as they combine various styles of fitness.

I still have designing or competing in a swim obstacle on my list to celebrate all the ways water is lifegiving.

Underwater Orienteering

Once above the surface obstacles have been tackled, how about upping the ante underwater? If you Scuba, underwater orienteering is an option that uses the route finding of surface orienteering in addition to specialized underwater wayfinding tools used in Scuba diving. In Scuba gear, participants find their way to each point underwater, often in set shape designs. If you are not Scuba-certified, don't worry. Try setting up a course where you can swim from checkpoint to checkpoint on a map. Or try a beach area where you can snorkel with a mask and fins from destination to destination. You could even include a diving or freediving point to navigate to within these options, keeping safety in mind. Combining these elements or inserting a water orienteering section in a multisport event is another way to incorporate the variants of existing sports into your own, in your chosen location and body of water.

Always Finish With Water

After all this, it probably comes as no surprise that one of my *other* core tenets of multisport is "Always Finish With Water."

I love finishing endurance events and training with water sports. Getting in the water provides refreshment, rejuvenation, can help recovery, and prevent things like ticks and poison ivy by getting wet and cleanish before leaving an event site. I used this tenet many times after racing through all manner of weather, heat, briars, brambles, bracken, and underbrush during off-road triathlons and adventure races.

It does not matter if it is an ocean, lake, river, stream, or pool, water helps. A long run, followed by a river kayak, followed by a pool swim is one of the most enjoyable ways to spend a day outside and finish with water. The water after the run, working the lower body, and the kayak, working the upper body is an ultimate treat. I add fins, a snorkel and mask, goggles, and water fitness tools to round out the multisport elements of the day, and family and children to keep kids involved and included in our human-powered water fun.

Volcanic Mountain, Desert, Jungle Trail/Water

After running up and down the volcanic mountains of the Canary Islands, I spent time rejuvenating with saltwater Thalasso water therapy and soaking in a weightless anti-gravity pool. Running across a desert upward of an ultramarathon each day for five days, through the ancient sands of Namibia, made me dream about jumping in the desert lodge's pool that, if I could survive, I would submerge myself in as soon as possible. Even running through the rainforests of New Zealand was not enough, I had to jump in a roaring river after that ultramarathon because I always liked to finish with even more water.

Yoga/Lake

A hot yoga class and a lake swim make for a wet combination of all day multisporting. Yes, your bathroom and deck will be full of towels, but that is a sign of a multisport life well-lived. Starting or ending my days in the summer with a kayak and swim in the lake, as the wind whips my face and hair and the water offers a magical life-affirming force of aqua, allows me to appreciate my surroundings and fuel my daily life ahead, towels and all.

Island Sail/Swim/Cave/Water

On a trip to Bermuda, Parker and I worked each day to create our own multisport experiences on the island. One day we sailed on a mini catamaran followed by a crisp, cold swim in the bright blue bay. We then hiked down into a cave to go caving, taking advantage of this area of the island's natural wonders. While underground, we swam again in an even colder cave pool before hiking back out and warming up in a hot tub. This mini multisport combination took place within a few hours of an afternoon and linked natural resources together to explore and experience the special offering of the island we were visiting. It also all centered around the water.

Snowshoe/XC Ski/Hot & Run/Ice Trail/Cold

One winter in Colorado, I spent the day snowshoeing and cross country skiing finished by a warm, reviving soak in the giant outdoor hot tub surrounded by mountains and snow. It was all water. Conversely, I often fill our outdoor stock tank pool in January and let it freeze in the low temperatures of winter. After runs and winter sports, we use the tank as a plunge pool to activate cryotherapy recovery principles. This cold-water therapy option keeps the fun in our backyard and gives winter its own seasonal post-exercise water session. Winter water therapy, be it hot or cold water, is the perfect coping mechanism for snow days and winter mix.

Hike/Lake

After hiking with our children in backpacks, we always include finishing with water as well. We try to plan our hikes and backpacking on trails that have lakes or rivers nearby. Then we take off our shoes and wade in the usually freezing water for instant refreshment before having a picnic or snack on the sand waterside, to fully take nature in, reflect and recover.

Destination & Journey

When I was training for my first marathon, I would run seven miles to a bakery and buy a scone afterward. Those runs seemed so long and so far. Finishing those early marathon training runs seemed possible only because I was ending them with breakfast; ending them somewhere. My route was safe, on sidewalks, exposed, and near people and traffic. My mom would pick me up after and I would crash on our drive home. Today, I laugh at those early runs and how long an easy hour run seemed at the time. But the fact that I was running to a café for scones I can still taste today, made my destination a part of my journey.

This concept, that the journey *is* the destination, can help you create and design your own multisport workouts. Some of my best destinations when training with various sports through the years include:

Running to a coffee shop grand opening in the freezing cold one winter. Since the event was during my run time and on my route, I decided to run there. Running through the city's center on an urban run took concentration and an extra layer of personal safety, but I liked being close to the action and exploring a downtown environment, even when that included backways and alleyways. I noticed the small details of the landscape around me in a new way when venturing via human power. The discovery of the little things on a frequently traveled route added a fine-point knowledge to a destination run.

Alternately, when a coffee shop opened on the opposite side of town in the suburbs, I ran there in summer's heavy heat, rewarding myself with an iced caffeinated version. The calm similarity of suburbia was a shock from the trails and urban hazards of my usual runs. I felt myself relax more on the wide open sidewalks now shaded by 20-year-old trees rather than my routine waterside 100-year-old cottonwoods.

I also like to run to coffee and bookstore story time during seasonal rains when no one else is out, choosing instead to shelter inside from the storms. If my husband and kids pick me up after they see me run along the way, this allows the children to feel part of our active lifestyle in an easy, accessible way, by them seeing us multisporting in any type of weather. What is more, they can do something fun of their own at the destination, while enjoying the journey.

Three ways of basic running—trails, urban and suburban—could be done alone or combined into one long run, which was usually my preference. Either way, running or multisporting to something infused my training and events with new elements of journeying.

In the summer, I like to run to a local farm-to-table café for blackberry lemonades or bike to a dessert shop along the bike trail with our kids in the chariot stroller behind us. Kayaking to the annual fireworks show or packrafting to a baseball game are other ideas. Need an oil change or your car worked on? Drive there and run, bike, or walk home, or vice versa. Sunday school training at church on Saturday mornings during run time? Run there. Cousin's volleyball game? Bike to it. Invited to a holiday gathering or birthday party? Run, bike, scooter or multisport there. This works best with close friends and relatives, as they will be most understanding when you arrive to the event sweaty, tired, immediately jump in the pool or lake, and must eat NOW. If something is too far away at first, drive halfway, park, and then go. Don't let obstacles stand in the way of your ideas. When you adopt the Destination Journey outlook of multisport, you can multisport and train to a destination, making your journey along the way part of your process. It is fun, an active way to participate in life that is already happening, and sets an example for others, including children, on how to reach places using your own internal engine, one of the best features of multisport!

Finding Your Own Passions

As you think more about how to multisport, you will develop your own tenets to include and build around. What are you drawn to? Start there. Biking, running, pedal kayaking, or skiing to a special, desired destination are motivators and tenets that inspire. Including freshness, like ziplining or kiteboarding on vacation, gives me ideas to plan around, as does trying a new sport from the list or finding a new one, or new progression of one. Remember the multisport tenet to use what you have around you at home or far away when traveling as you add fun, challenge, and exploration to your world via multisport. Be adaptable. Be resourceful. Make multisport work for you.

Overlanding

The tradition of overlanding celebrates the great around-the-world routes by land: Cape to Cairo though Africa, Alaska to

Patagonia along North America to South America via the Pan-American Highway, and London to Asia across Europe to the Far East.

Explorers have taken these routes via foot, bicycle, motorcycle, and vehicle, as well as combinations of each to chart new ways for travel and journeying.

Overlanding today is a way to explore the outdoors via vehicle travel, camping and often self-sufficiency.

Overlanding has deep traditions that help us cross continents in a multiple of conveyances, something we can't ignore when collecting the history and ways to multisport. By studying the traditional and new ways to circle the globe, chasing heights and depths, we can delve even more into the extreme with my favorite, the self-propelled versions.

Modern adventurers have found ways to cross intercontinental byways via skateboard, inline skates, and scooters; SUPing lengths of rivers; swimming around countries; pedaling oceans; and crossing deserts via bikes with sails called whikes. They set world-records journeying around the world using only human power, circumnavigating without fossil fuels.

Around the world yacht racing is sailing's answer to the around the world challenge. Ocean rowing includes the four oceans of the Atlantic, Pacific, Indian and Arctic where rowers cross the entirety by human power solo or with groups of pairs, fours and six-member crews. The fifth Southern Ocean has also now been crossed most recently by human-powered rowing across the Drake Passage from Cape Horn to the Antarctic Peninsula.

Whatever journey you partake in, the spirit of a travel adventure lives in multisport. Classic overland and ocean journeys prove our mettle and that we were born to travel by our own propulsion.

38 by 8: Eight Sports in Eight Days

Roller Skiing, Strollerblading, Swimming, Scootering, Trekking, Gravel Biking, Packrafting & Running

On my 36th birthday, I had just returned home from the hospital with my newborn daughter. I was up all night, similar to past late night and early morning birthday multisport events, but of a very different nature. Emotions were high as we tried to survive those overwhelming early days of new parenthood.

For 37, I was about five months pregnant with my son Lachlan. I did manage to run seven miles, for 37 years, and spent a day at the lake with Parker for stand up paddleboarding, openwater swimming with fins for added adventure, and swimming while pulling our boards in the lake.

As I neared 38 years, not quite out of the maternity phase of my life, I was longing for a multisport adventure that would accommodate my days at home with the children and my writing and work schedule, but still capture the energy of a transglobal self-propelled overland expedition.

Enter 38 by 8: Eight Sports in Eight Days.

Eight Sports in Eight Days was a self-generated, self-propelled family adventure with an international book theme, *Around the World in 80 Days*, itself an overland and sea journey, to tie it all together. Each day, for eight days in a row, I chose a new sport to participate in on the eight days leading up to my 38th birthday. I wanted to link human-powered endurance sports, history, travel, exploration, books, and adventure in a wild, creative, multisport way.

Day 1: Roller Ski

It was a warm spring morning, so on Day One, I woke up before my husband and children were awake for roller skiing with my cross country skates that mimic cross country skis. I used the accompanying poles to balance myself and made sure to wear gloves, a helmet, and typical inline skate protection pads for safety as I rolled along the blacktop in the cloudy blue May morning. Instead of relying on snow for movement, the rollers on the bottom of the ski skates allowed me to XC train during the non-snow months. I love cross country skiing. It is a total body workout and perfect for an outdoor endurance athlete. The only problem is I don't get to do it as often as I like living where I do, versus somewhere with lots of snow and groomed ski paths. The roller option was a great way for me to try a new-to-me, self-propelled sport that I could do in my own neighborhood and integrate into my multisport arsenal. I felt ready to tackle the day and the multisports ahead by kicking off Eight Sports in Eight Days with an enjoyable new sports option.

Day 2: Strollerblade

Due to work and family commitments, I saved Day Two's multisport event for a late afternoon inline skate after my workday.

I donned my Rollerblades leftover from my Rollerblade racing days as a 10-year-old. I saved them and enjoyed breaking them out every now and then to cross-train or use in adventure racing. Again, one of the lessons of multisport is to use what you have. You don't have to have all new gear. Sure, new inline skates would be amazing, but these would do for the time being and it was fun to find new ways to use old things. I added my pads and helmet and broke out the Thule stroller for two with the jogging attachment. I was Strollerblading. Stollerblading is Rollerblading (inline skating) with a stroller. It is super fun. It is also a wonderful way to involve your child or children in your multisport workout. After the kids were loaded and strapped into all their age-appropriate harnessing, off we went for a skate around our neighborhood. We all liked feeling the breeze as we switched gears from our day to evening routine. One of the things that is thrilling about Storllerblading is that you often feel steadier by holding on to the stroller bar. This felt different than simply Rollerblading. It was both more comfortable, as I skated faster, but more jarring, as I balanced speed and safety for the children's sake.

Day 3: Swim

It was time for an early morning wake-up on Day Three. I would have loved to do an open-water swim this time of year instead, but I did not have time to mess with a wetsuit, daylight, an open-water swim buddy, or drive time to my open-water swim location. I needed the fastest, most efficient option and that was my closest pool. This solo workout felt good, freeing, and comfortable; and easy option with a core sport, one of my originals from tri days, for midweek.

Day 4: Scooter

Another early morning. As hard as it is to wake up, early morning workouts are my favorite way to start the day. However, this one was different than my usual Thursday morning training session. I was going scootering! Electric scooters had their moment, but I used my old-fashioned kick scooter designed for covering rough terrain and long distances in adventure racing. Scootering brought out my inner kid and reminded me of my days romping around my neighborhood growing up collecting flora and fauna. As an adult it made me happy and free as I kicked and slid along the bike path. It wasn't a bike I had spent hours on. It was faster than walking and running. Like skating, it was just plain fun. I liked how I used different leg muscles to balance and kick myself along. This was one benefit of multisport right here: escaping the traditional; the routine; trying something new; working your body in new ways; tapping into that curiosity of a child and going for it by your own propulsion. Scootering it turned out, was a beautiful way to start your day. I was thankful that during my adventuring racing days, one of the events called for a scooter, and that I decided to resurrect this wheeled transport and add it into my multisport lifestyle. Adding a scooter pre- or post- other endurance training was a way to integrate freedom into daily life, even if not crossing the entire United States by scooter like some intrepid adventurers, I could still benefit and enjoy a kick-scooter jaunt now and then.

Day 5: Trek with Two

It was Friday evening. What better way to kick off our weekend than taking the children on a hike by the river? With them strapped to me. I wore my oldest, Penelope, on my back in an Osprey hiking backpack and my youngest, Lachlan, on my front in a Baby Bijorn carrier. It was empowering to walk freely with both children on my person. I felt like an ancient nomad following the season, animals, and plants for food, camp and life. While slower than normal trekking and more cumbersome, I liked exploring multisport with my children and family. We were born for movement and self-propelled travel and this event cemented that.

Day 6: Gravel Bike Circumnavigation

I saved my longest, most time-consuming event for the weekend when I had the most time and family support. My mom watched our children and Parker, my dad, and I set off on a 38-mile gravel bike for my 38 years. This was not a typical gravel bike, however. It was a circumnavigation exploring our city's inner core. I wanted to link a series of bike paths, routes, and streets to circle the entire central area of our town, and claim our sense of place. From South, to East, to North, to West, we circled the city riding through urban areas. We passed rivers, canals, and streams. This biketouring gave us a reason to urbex new areas around our very own town that we often bisected by car. It was raining for much of the ride and that added to our element of excitement with the feel of being out in it having an adventure. Rather than simply driving across town, we were biking across it. Now whenever we see the paths that we took that day while traveling on the highway, we know that we biked there. We know how the routes flow and link and take us back home. This gives us ownership of the land around us and begs us to learn and discover even more along the way. Oh, the things we found on that ride; ones that were there all along, we only had to take the time to see them.

Day 7: Packraft

We again took advantage of weekend time and childcare to have a day date on the river for Day Seven with Packrafting. Parker and I took to the water for a paddle close to home followed by recovery time (*Always Finish With Water*) in the pool with the kids for an all-around water day. The packrafts are lighter than traditional kayaks. With the Kansas wind, this made for a slower and more challenging paddle than we would normally have had with our heavier boats. This change up of watercraft was a benefit of multisport and allowed us a novelty and added pizzaz to our comfortable paddle route.

Day 8: 3.8-Mile Run

For my last day, Day Eight, my actual 38th birthday, I woke up before dawn and ran an easy 3.8 miles, meeting my dad at our midpoint bridge. Running was the simplest and often hardest of the sports, so it was a fitting end cap to my event. I was exhausted. But it turned out I just once again had mastitis. Ahh new motherhood and multisport. No one said it would be easy. The sports once again proved a needed emotional release from parenting.

I didn't have the bandwidth to devote long hours to multi-sport this year, and I couldn't be away from my son for too many hours at a time, so I designed a multisport around my unique needs at this exact point in my life. Some days I could wake up early for a sport. Others I did in the evening with my children. I saved my longest bout for the weekend and incorporated others to join in the fun, and even integrated a day date with some help on childcare. I made the flexibility of multisport work for me. Including friends and family made it all more worthwhile and rewarding in the end.

38 by 8: Eight Sports in Eight Days was a challenge of sport, timing, energy, and logistics, but it also allowed me to go out and keep exploring new paths in my city and create my own fun. I was able to escape the traditional and the routine with a custom-generated overland multisport.

Family Integrations

One of the ideal things about multisport is that it can include partners, parents and children together. When our children were young, we loved coming up with ways to pair them into our multisport lifestyle and still do.

Bike/Paddle/Swim/Bike

One of our favorite family multisports includes a family bike ride to grandma's house with the children in the bike stroller. We can make this route short by going straight there, or longer by adding in miles on the bike trail. We can even divide the children into one stroller pulled by Parker and one pulled by myself, or we can alternate who pulls the double stroller for prolonged endurance and rotated power training.

Once we arrive, Parker and I hop in our kayaks to paddle on the river while the children play with their grandmother. We then all swim in the pool together before biking back home.

Family Triathlon: Bike/Hike/Run

We also came up with a Family Triathlon where one day we biked with the children in the bike chariot stroller, hiked with them in backpacks, then followed that by running with them in the jogging stroller. We even included the Siberian husky on the hiking portion for a full family event.

Multisporting with the stroller provided endless new adventures to be had and even more cardio combos. The hiking backpacks allowed us to take the children to one of our adventure grounds and multisport zones and hike the trails of Colorado, among many other treasured destinations.

Running Games

When I was young my family invented a game called Strong Golf. Kansas specializes in the extremes of suffocating or freezing. To survive the boiling summers full of roaring heat and crackling grass with a dry smell all its own, we often ran in the evenings or early mornings, around our neighborhood golf course. With only occasional light winds to buff the skin, enduring the purifying swelter of running during a Kansas summer, spotting the golf course sprinklers shooting cold water was an inspiration.

How could we stay away? The possibility of revival was too tempting. We must run through the sprinklers; to get in; to get wet and help us keep running! As night would fall, we would run onto the golf course, running from each sprinkler to each sprinkler, sprinting in between for interval training. Instead of hitting a golf ball to each tee, we ran to each, and rewarded ourselves with a dash through the oscillating sprinkler, powerful, pressurized and invigorating. Strong Golf was an early example of multisport, combining two sports together, running intervals between sprinklers on a golf course, that was perfect and fun for kids of all ages. I still play Strong Golf today when I need a dash of energy and happiness to keep running.

Multisport with children needs more gear, more time, more patience, and much more food, water, and fuel, but we learned we were just getting started on our next journey. As long as we were looking for new challenges, exploring, and finding fun, we knew we would always keep multisporting.

The Ultra Trifecta: 100-Mile Bike, Run & Kayak

When you create your own expeditions and events around multisport, there will be barriers. Anyone who is pushing a multitude of boundaries, from the physical, mental, emotional, to the family, work, life balance, will encounter obstacles along the way. This is what it feels like to walk the edge; to be revolutionary and radical.

I created and designed a 100-mile kayak expedition to complete my goal of covering 100 miles in three individual sports: biking, running and paddling. As an ultrarunner who ran 100 miles, and also biked 100 miles, my new goal was now paddling 100 miles at one go, in one day, in the same form and spirit as an ultrarun or century bike, with no rest breaks, only quick transitions at each checkpoint for bathroom breaks and refueling.

I coined this distance event the Ultra Trifecta. Striving for my Ultra Trifecta goal was important to me because it would make me an ultra-endurance multisport athlete in three distinct sports. I wasn't simply an ultrarunner. Or an Ironman bike rider. Or a casual recreational paddler. By reaching 100 miles in three separate sports, I would further test and prove the concept of multisport by going the 100-mile distance in three categories.

100-Mile Bike

I completed my first 100-mile century road bike ride during my triathlon and adventure racing days. I used it as a training ride, and it took just under seven hours to complete. It was a humid day and my phone died from the heat. Riding through small towns that still had metal HOT and COLD water towers let me explore the back roads outside my city in a new, but still human-powered way. The ride began in the early morning dark, and encompassed light, hills, flats, sun, clouds, rain, wind, thunder and, always a favorite on the bike, lightning, as I had to escape an incoming storm by dashing for shelter under a hay barn. It was not my first or last time to do this while exploring, training, and racing in Kansas.

One such race was at an Ironman 70.3. After a combative lake swim, it began to storm heavily on the biking portion of the event. On the back roads in Northeast Kansas biking alone, as often happens when competitors spread out over the course, the thunder boomed, and the lightning flashed. I was separated from the other riders along the 56-mile bike leg through crop fields and winding hills. My bike shoes filled with water from the torrential rain and overflowed onto the rest of my soaking body as water gushed down my legs. My wet hands gripped my handlebars and breaks through my bike gloves and slid when I went over bumps. Sheet lightning flashed through the sky. I began to worry. But I kept pedaling and navigating the course. I was wearing a spandex racing outfit of a tank top and bike shorts, but at the last minute in the transition area, after checking the day's weather and potential for storms, I threw in a lightweight wind jacket that I had donned at the swim/ bike transition. As it plastered my wet body, and I rode my bike through a lightning storm, I was so thankful for the small amount of warmth it provided, without I would be a shivering mess. It clung to me in the humid spring storm as the skies blackened overhead.

Then, hope miraculously arrived around the next bend! A race organizer parked a truck on the side of the road and was ushering racers atop their bikes into a nearby hay barn to wait out the storm. Salvation! Safety! Shivers. Not many other racers had added a drag-inducing layer to their spandex. I was forever thankful that I had, as many lost body heat fast as they huddled against the hay, cold and shaking. I was too, but I was mercifully prepared with my lifesaving blue windbreaker. After about 45 minutes, the skies gave way to sun and the riders piled back out of the barn and onto more hills and the rest of the race. Afterward, upon arriving back to the bike/run transition, we found that the grassy plain and included transition gear floated away in the flash flood. If those events were not exciting enough, our SUV had become stuck in the mud. It along with all the others parked in the flooded fields had to be towed out of the race site by a team of professional tow truckers.

While leading up to covering the 100-mile bike distance, I designed bike routes that explored and linked country dirt roads, including the historic Kansas Flint Hills and Coronado Heights, where Coronado the famous Spanish conquistador led an expedition in the 1500s. I embraced the juxtaposition of being in the country on a bike: The old, tactile, and natural, and the new, metallic, and shiny. I was often riding in the rain as I pedaled through the sparse counties, always on guard to bike fast away from the areas where farm guard dogs lived and liked to give chase. When it wasn't raining, my routes usually ended up including an additional water segment like creek crossing, in bike shoes. Wet gap crossings were a constant no matter the sport. I hoisted my bike up in one hand, balancing with the other, wading through the mud and muck, then continued through the small towns on the rim of the city, gaining adventure racing experience as I tackled water crossings along the way, taking the ideas behind urban exploring and using them in the countryside.

Biking 100 miles, along with training and racing through the state, was an entry into long-distance, multi-hour events and base building sessions for all distance sports. From climbing mountains that took weeks to summit, to marathon swimming, ultrarunning, and long treks, building the base for long-distance multisports began with lots of bike training.

100-Mile Run

My first 100-mile run was an ultrarun in 2012. After my first marathon, I jumped into the world of ultrarunning. I built my distance training starting with a 50k, progressing to a 50-miler, then a 100k, followed by a 100-miler. My first 100-mile run took just over a day to complete. Compared to biking and paddling 100 miles at once, running was by far the most challenging and the most demanding on all fronts. The physical toil, the mental fortitude, and the training dedication all took more when it came to running.

After my first 100-mile run, I began competing in ultras around the world and multi-day, stage racing events. Once I completed an ultrarun on five of the seven continents, I wanted to get back to the water and focus on more paddling. I hoped to run on the other two continents of Asia and Antarctica someday, but in the meantime, I heeded the call of the water.

I boarded my old family kayak and started designing multisport days with paddling sports while investing in more specialized boats. Kayaking, packrafting, canoeing, stand up paddleboarding, and rafting were all paddling variations I was excited to explore more and integrate into my multisport workouts and events. The more ways and means I could find to paddle, meant more variety, fun, challenge, and adventure on and off the water.

After several endurance kayak events, and my long-distance birthday kayak, I set a goal of going even farther. I wanted to kayak 100 miles and become an ultrapaddler multisporter.

100-Mile Kayak

I have always been a runner and a swimmer. In a different way I have always been a waterwoman as well. My boating history is just as rich, but rather than being a focal- point sport, it ebbed and flowed like the rivers around me.

Perhaps a program through the park department in my hometown is to thank for me being drawn to such a variety of watercraft. One summer, I participated in a camp that introduced kids to different boats on the Little Arkansas River. This introduction as a young person gave me experience on various boats and a reference point for adventure racing and then multisport in years to come. We learned to sail small sailboat dinghies, how to row in an eight-person scull, how to kayak, and how to canoe. It was a week of multisport for paddling variations.

My family owned a canoe and I competed in festival canoe races with friends when travel schedules allowed. We also went whitewater rafting in Colorado on family vacations. After River Kids camp, we bought a family kayak as well, quickly tipping it and falling in our river headfirst, upon its first use. I gained more exposure to rowing through a river program as well that let me try the scull boats and be part of a crew team. I would go on to sail in the Caribbean, row eights, fours, twos, and singles in college, and train in canoes in school and at Outward Bound. Later I would also gain whitewater kayaking experience and add new forms of boating, like building our own rafts, stand up paddleboarding and packrafting. These each empowered me to expand my sport options and range for multisport.

The early boat exposure and growing up around water allowed me to be comfortable with any boat thrown my way in adventure racing, where I often had to paddle long distances in flimsy inflatable, sit-on-top kayaks and wear bulky life vests. I also enjoyed finding new sorts of boats, like outriggers, and gaining more sailing training.

Being a waterwoman on the Plains is not a given, as I am constantly on the hunt for water, just like my ancestors, but it has been a lifelong dedication to the waters and ways to interact and be in them.

With this history in mind, the 100-Mile Ultrapaddle was not only about the distance, or the multisport combo. Something inside me knew I could do it and that I had to try.

Have you ever felt that way about an event or sport? If so, this might be your starting point for your own multisport endurance challenge.

Nearly five years in the making, the 100-Mile Ultrapaddle came together in the spring of 2022. As soon as I could be away from my young son, I knew it was time for ultramarathon kayak training to begin. While I had to set my goals aside for a while, the big idea of a 100-mile, non-stop paddle stayed with me and motivated me through the trials of early parenthood and COVID-19.

I first researched rivers throughout the United States, up and down North America, and across the globe to find an ultrapaddle event that met my requirements. No such event existed, so I designed and created my own 100-mile paddling expedition. Like the multisport events before, when I couldn't find what I was looking for in distance, challenge, time, location, and overall spirit, I created my own that worked for me and my specific goal.

After studying rivers for paths that would allow me to paddle without portage, locks, or dams, and 100 miles at the same time, I settled on four Midwestern rivers to consider: the Arkansas River, the Little Arkansas River, the Kansas River, and the Missouri River. Each week, I observed and collected water and weather data, and I studied the historical information needed to plan a safe, successful expedition.

Multisport life is not for the faint of heart. Balancing the training aspects, research, and logistics required taking on new levels of dedication. The 100-Mile Ultrapaddle preparation was all-consuming.

Parker, my kayaking partner, and I faced weekly obstacles. The children were sick. We all were sick. We paddled on. Our time was pressed, the weather was insane. It rained, it hailed, it melted us with humidity one week, sunburning us the next, and freezing us in between. The wind knocked against us. The river froze over. Rapids soaked us, and then out of nowhere, the very next day, the Little Arkansas River was lowered making one of our training grounds impossible to navigate.

The changing environments and weather conditions offered new experiences on rivers I had boated on my entire life and peppered me with resilience for the ultrapaddle ahead. Meanwhile, every event possible from funerals to high school reunions, to work events and conferences, happened during the training cycle, but we pushed on. We had to have plans A, B, C, D, and backups. Each day was something new to overcome. We switched between rivers, back and forth on the Big Arkansas and the Little, and alternated our watercrafts, changing boats to best suit the situation of the day, including water levels and conditions.

I located, checked out, and studied academic literature on the history of my rivers from libraries and bought others as I, more than ever before on past river expeditions, studied routes, Native American plant, animal, and survival knowledge, the role in pioneer settlements along historic westward trails, and the life that the watersheds feed, even taking my children on field trips to river exhibits to get them involved early as fellow guardians of our rivers. We planned future family backpacking trips to the source and travels back down the riverbends.

All the while, we studied gear lists and gathered the innumerable items we needed for an expedition on the river for 100 miles. I pulled equipment from each of my past multisports to put together exactly what I needed on this specific undertaking. Not being part of an organized event or race meant that we alone were responsible for our food, water, gear, and most of all, our own personal safety.

As the seasons changed, I narrowed my potential rivers to two. The Little Arkansas was convenient for paddle training, but not a long-distance, navigable option. We followed it in and out of town on long narrow paddles that took us though backyards and under overpasses as silent travelers paddling below the highways and byways above. These intercity distractions were nice for weekends or evenings, but not cut out for the long 100-mile haul.

The Kansas River is the largest tributary of the Missouri River, one of the world's longest prairie rivers, and recreationally provides the Kansas Water Trail. However, the Kaw was salted with sandbars and low water, making a 100-mile paddle near impossible. It would even be challenging to go 100 miles on a week-long overnight camping trip on this river. Floaters would paddle short amounts each day then camp and sleep overnight. I didn't want this option. I wanted to get everything done at once. Fast and efficient. No stopping. The Kansas River united the university towns of both Parker and me, plus his birthplace of Kansas City. Paddling 100 miles on the Kaw would have been meaningful, uniting and home-state-based. However, the Kansas River was not to be, either.

Spring brought less precipitation than normal, so I ultimately had to change my target river from the Big Arkansas River to the Missouri River. I was sad that like the Kaw, the Arkansas River would have too many sandbars and not nearly enough water to paddle 100 miles in one day. The water levels at the start were less than one foot deep. Resigned, I steeled myself for the muddy Missouri. The Arkansas River was gone for this event, but not forgotten. I still had nearly 1,500 miles of the Arkansas River that I could keep exploring in some way, someday, perhaps even with the children and a variety of watercraft options and multisport ideas in tow.

It was on to the Missouri River, the longest river in the United States. To learn more about and prepare for the new Missouri River paddle expedition, I studied the Missouri, quickly with this month-out change in plans. I bought more books and further learned how to paddle and navigate this commercially trafficked river safely and follow Coast Guard maritime laws for night paddling and mapping the current. The U.S. Coast Guard would not know I was coming, unlike other organized events on the Missouri River. The river would be open, alive, and in its natural full flow element when I paddled it.

Paddling on the river always makes me feel united with the early American romance and reliance on rivers for commerce and connection. This was a trip of my own, in the vein of my river book collection of famous explorers charting new waters and adventurers trekking though jungles and paddling rapids on historic river quests. It was also another chapter in my study of Americana and what makes us frontiers people. I read my children historic river picture books, gathered living American history experiences to have along the trip, and found ways to integrate the wild frontier that the Missouri River and Louis and Clark's Journey of Discovery beckoned. The early exploration of the Missouri River served in part as an economic justification for Thomas Jefferson's Louisiana Purchase.

We read up on Mike Fink of the keelboaters who floated downstream and then used long poles and ropes to haul new-American wooden river boats back upstream full of cargo. I had grown up a fan of Paul Bunyan and Davy Crockett, heroes and legends of untamed America. Mike Fink was of similar fame and known as King of the Keelboaters and King of the River. The keelboat of Lewis and Clark's initial journey was similar. I sang about the Erie Canal as we also read up on canal history and modern treks on the former foot paths. These myths around America's great rivers shaped my consciousness as a child, feeding off shows from the 1950s that aired on the Disney Chanel in the 1990s and schoolbook history on the American West. The 100-Mile Ultrapaddle was my manifestation of that consciousness coming alive, with my children and family involved as well, as I worked toward this capstone multisport 100-mile goal.

Ultrapaddle day arrived. My team consisted of Parker and my dad who would alternate driving, crewing and kayaking. Not wanting to be away from our young children any more than necessary, we went to bed at 7 PM at home once dropping them at my mom's and packing Parker's Jeep with our food, water, supplies, equipment, and boat gear. We then slept and rested for a few hours before an alpine start of waking back up at 11 PM. We borrowed this alpine start knowledge from my years mountaineering and climbing mountains like Kilimanjaro in Africa, Mt. Elbrus in Russia, and Mt. Rainer in the United States.

After loading the two kayaks on top of the car in the dark, we took off for Jefferson City, the capital of Missouri. We began the kayak expedition there after driving five hours listening to *Undaunted Courage*, a classic river book that we all owned, to tap into the proper feeling of an expedition on the Missouri. Once we arrived, we set up, and packed the boats that Parker and my dad would rotate paddling in, while the other drove to the next boat ramp, as I would paddle continuously. The access points served as our checkpoints along the route 100 miles downstream.

With a waterside view of the state capital building, I set off downriver and paddled 18 hours straight to reach 100 miles along the Wide Missouri.

I would like to say it was safe and easy, but the Big Muddy presented its challenges. Wing dikes, sand dredges, barges, flying carp, bridge pilings, fast-moving water, can buoys, crossing beacons, river debris, channel finding, current following, night-time fog, dark wayfinding, high water, navigation charts, and more were new hurdles to overcome when paddling this commercially viable river.

I did, however, welcome the history it brought and the introduction it provided us to the historic East as a gateway to the West.

We sang *Oh Shenandoah*, the theme song from fur traders traveling down the Missouri of old and paddled next to modern day trains carrying freight across the country. I thought about the early American pole boater's impossible work and Sacagawea who was nursing an infant as she guided Lewis and Clark on their voyage in long wooden pirogue canoes.

Some of my favorite moments from the 100-Mile Ultra-paddle include coming into the historic river towns at night and seeing their twinkling lights as beacons of respite; spotting Parker at a checkpoint ramp, the lone light in total darkness, again a welcomed, comforting sign in the black night on the water; paddling at sunset and feeling a part of something greater as I kayaked next to a cross country freight train chugging westward; and intensely focusing on the light fog that seemed frighteningly formidable as night descended. Multisport allowed me to propel myself through the waters of the Missouri River exploring and living life large along the way.

It was an overcast day at the end of May, perfect for paddling and avoiding too much sun exposure. I wore a pair of old trail running shoes that had holes rubbed in the netting on the top of the shoe. They were perfect for paddling shoes as those holes lent a natural draining feature. I like wearing shoes I can hike in to paddle in case of an emergency where I have to evacuate the river and trek to safety. When paddling prairie rivers at home, shallows were a given, and I often had to exit my boat and drag it across sandbanks, so solid shoes that could get wet and dry quickly were a must for me.

Also drawing from the old pile, I wore some of my first rain gear, in muddy river green, from teenage backpacking days that these days now featured more as wind gear. While this event took a lot of gear on one hand, I also enjoyed using the gear I had to accomplish my goals as simply as possible. I saved my heavy-duty rain gear in my drybag in my kayak hatch for emergencies. It was a mental comfort that I did so.

As the sun set the cool day turned downright cold. I wore close fitting tech shorts through the morning and day, topped by my green river wind pants that were soaked from water splashed the entire time. By evening, I changed into water pants that were like quick-drying yoga pants under my wind pants. For my top layer, I wore a light-colored, long sleeve water top with my green zip wind jacket the whole day.

I added a visor to keep the sun off my face, and kayak gloves to prevent paddling blisters. I also had to wear my custom Go Far book Buff around my neck and a fleece headband on my ears to stay warm as night crept around the bends. Despite it being a mild May day in the 60s, it was cold on the water, especially at night when the sun finally descended for good beyond the horizon in a blazing orange streak.

As night fell around me, the temperatures dropped even more, and I didn't want to stop paddling. At our boat ramp checkpoints, I hopped in and out quickly to move my legs, but

I was eager to keep paddling and moving to say warm while generating body heat. We attached our red, green, and white lights required for night boating on the Missouri by the Coast Guard and entered the next phase of the paddle.

My finish of 100 miles was planned at the Daniel Boone Bridge. Daniel Boone was a famous American frontiersman. The Boonslick is a cultural region of Missouri along the river that played an important part in America's expansion. The Boone's Lick Road was the primary way for westward settlers. Where it ended the Santa Fe Trail began. The Santa Fe Trail followed the Arkansas River through central Kansas. Here our rivers and this journey met together over history and pioneers.

Once I reached 100 miles of ultramarathon kayaking at the Daniel Boon Bridge in the dead of night however, I had to keep paddling 11 more miles as there was no access ramp, way out of the water, or connection back to civilization.

I had to activate my adapting strategy that is key in expedition-length multisport. Having an adapting strategy means having your plans, your backup plans, and your contingency plans in place. Just like in 100-Mile Ultrapaddle training, I had to be flexible and mentally fit to keep going even when I wanted to stop, as I had already reached my 100-mile distance goal.

I knew I would eventually be able to exit the water. I knew I could keep going. I had to be nimble and adaptable, even more than I wanted to be, even more than I was prepared to be on this paddling day. It felt dangerous, the cold night fog, with only a paddling partner for company, on a highly trafficked river. I had to put those thoughts aside, and those of aching to be done. Instead, I had to adapt and refocus my strategy to complete my goal safely and correctly, finishing strong and intact, while remaining calm.

An adapting strategy is a huge part of any distance event and even more important in multisport with so many moving parts in play. Any piece could collide at any time. As a participant, I had to stay fluid, living, and acting in real time.

I changed my process, internal self-talk, and thoughts to better suit my current situation—one of not being able to exit the water. We crept slowly by the dark banks searching for a small off-flow area for a potential exit we had spotted on the maps. However, the potential idea was just that, an idea, a theory, something to try. We tried it and it didn't work, so we had to move on. By adapting, I could better survive and function within my current environment of black, cold, continual kayaking.

Twenty plus hours in, paddling in the dark, I was ready to stop being on. However, I had to find a way to keep paddling. Having extra food and water with me gave me the confidence to paddle even when I was physically tired, sleepy, cold, and sore, knowing as long as I kept eating and drinking, I could make it through, based on past ultra and multisport experiences.

I adapted to the situation, by eating, drinking, and mentally relaxing as much as possible, when desperately searching for someway way off the river that wasn't the next bridge I had targeted on my map as a backup. By shifting this focus, I could do what needed to be done, allowing me to complete the 100-Mile Ultrapaddle successfully. This was not guaranteed. Any number of things could have happened that were out of my control. I am thankful that everything came together to complete the event. Expeditions in nature are never a given. They are always a gift.

Knowing that I had dry clothes in my kayak hatch also helped propel me forward. I knew if I stopped, I would be so cold from the dark, damp, fog, and night that I would freeze instantly. In fact, I was already probably too cold for comfort, but the constant need to paddle to go anywhere kept me from becoming too chilly. I knew that if we stopped before we had ramp access, I would immediately have to strip down and change my base layers and top them with my mountain-grade rain and water resistant shells. I even had my bivy sack and emergency blanket that I felt just might be called into play if we stopped for too long.

We learned from other Missouri paddlers that a night on the Missouri after a paddle is freezing cold. I packed a big travel down blanket in the crew Jeep and our sleeping bags if an emergency, waterside sleep was required. I imagined it being miserable and damp, reminding me of how I felt hiking up the Grand Canyon after running across and back, dreaming of stopping, but knowing that the discomfort of movement was easier than the effort required to stay warm after an unplanned stop.

I learned how to set aside thoughts, ideas, and feelings that were not moving me forward through ultra endurance events and multisport over my years as a multidisciplinary athlete. I was used to being alone with my own thoughts and to keep pushing onward. On the river, I embraced the situation, found the best, tried to enjoy the experience, or at least the memory that would come from it, and pushed on using the skills amassed from years as an endurance multisport athlete. Having an adapting strategy as I paddled allowed me to stay focused and malleable in whatever way was called for at the time.

I officially exited the water at the next bridge downstream at 3 AM Monday morning after 21 hours of kayaking. We finished along the Katy Trail, the same one that was where we began upstream as well. It was a sign of more family multisport adventures to come in Missouri for bikepacking and living history explorations along the historic river towns.

One of those towns was Chamois, Missouri, where I raced my first ultrarun in 2009 in the Spirit of the Osage 50k. Ultrarunning and ultrapaddling met in Missouri on paths I never dreamed I would be on, until one day, there I was. Making this strange coincidence even more thematic was that the chamois, a European mountain goat, was one of Parker's and my favorite animals, encountered face-to-face climbing via ferratas in the Italian Alps on our honeymoon. The town of Chamois, Missouri, is named for this animal. Our children have a stuffed animal version at home. These different multisport experiences were once again unifying our life and stories.

The MVP of the ultrapaddle, in addition to my teammates and old, used boating gear, ended up being a giant tub of pretzels I bought before the event. I went food shopping, loading up on my traditional bars and nut butters, but I was looking for that one thing that would raise my spirits and make the task of staying fueled for a day's worth of constant endurance paddling easier.

Borrowing from the multisport food and hydration systems guidelines, having a small motivator like a special food item could be essential. I saw the oversized plastic jar of peanut butter pretzels and knew that was it. When biking 100 miles, where the day is short and quick, I didn't need that kind of fuel. When running 100 miles, I required only light, tested, easily digestible foodstuff. But paddling 100 miles could call for peanut butter pretzel pillows. Those pretzels fueled us all during that day of paddling, delighted the children when we returned, and kept on giving as I turned the jar into an outside play aquarium afterward.

I had found that something—just a small thing, really—that added a fun element to the expedition. Having something that I don't normally eat, something to look forward to, had provided me with the unexpected. By having these pretzels with me, I was able to keep going when I wanted to stop and stay confident that I could keep paddling. They allowed me to practice my adapting strategy when things became tough, as they most inevitably will during multisport. This snack choice is an example of a little thing that can empower long multisport days that is actually a big thing in the overall view. Once you find your MVP, carry that power with you and use it on and off your multisport course.

Another reason that I paddled the Missouri River when and where I did, leaving on a Saturday night and starting on a Sunday morning, was that I was invited to an event in St. Charles, Missouri, that I needed to be at Monday afternoon. I could catch a quick post-paddle nap, but real sleep would have to wait. Paddling the Missouri made sense if I had to be in Missouri already. I paddled 100 miles stopping just before my event location at the Portage des Sioux in the area where the Missouri, Illinois, and Mississippi Rivers come together. It all felt fitting for my own discovery tour along the river. We planned to start

100 miles upstream and reach where I needed to be by human paddle power.

It was also the weekend of my 39th birthday. Would my birthday weekends ever be free from multisport? It was not likely. My birthday and multisport went hand in hand.

With that said, multisport and this ultrapaddle were not my life. They were *part* of my life, and I looked to fit them in when, where and how I could. Multisport enhances my life and gives me something to plan and work around, adding cohesiveness and tying of outside things together. Multisport united things in my life, but outside of it I was still able to be a wife and a mom among the other hybrid titles. Multisport allowed me to live multifacetedly and harmoniously regarding whatever my situation was. Instead of taking over my life, multisport gave me a way to complement it through internal engine power. People asked me if I would continue to adventure after having children. My answer was, absolutely! I just completed a huge ultra goal of paddling 100 miles continuously. I did this by following multisport concepts and using multisport ideals to fit my kayaking goal in my life, and as it happened, on the way to a destination.

Our endpoint of St. Charles, Missouri, was founded in 1769. Post-paddle, Parker and I took in the National Historic District that preserves the area's rich river heritage with many restored Federal-style brick colonial buildings along with early French and Spanish vestiges. St. Charles was an important supply point for the steamboat trade and the earliest westbound adventurers into the untamed territory beyond.

One on my goals of the 100-Mile Ultrapaddle was, like multisport, to explore my own geography and area pioneer history.

I wanted to accomplish the 100 miles of kayaking close to my home, in my own environment. This version of paddle did not exist before, so I created it. Borrowing the elements of creating my own multisport, I made an expedition that had meaning in a multitude of ways for me. It added fun, a challenge, and a new watershed to explore. In addition to the distance of 100 miles of non-stop paddling, I was able to experience America's river history along the way.

I was grateful for the rivers, waterways, and possibilities as I met my goal and traveled a previously unknown journey. I felt connected with the early Americans and the self-sufficient, forward-looking spirit of frontier peoples.

This Ultra Trifecta, through-the-years multisport combination, of a 100-mile road bike, a 100-mile ultrarun, and now a 100-mile kayak, brought new challenges, arenas, and histories to explore, and fun to all our worlds.

This capstone, expedition-length multisport series solidified for me the importance of finding experiences that pushed comfort levels and moved goals forward, multifaceted, complex and rewarding that they were. Multisport allowed us to meld it all together.

Multisport gave me a way to ask what was possible, seek new limits, test those limits, and push beyond them. It taught me new skills, building on a lifetime of amassment, as I tried new sports, new routes, new destinations, and new combinations of each as a life-long outdoor athlete and adventurer. Multisport allowed me to follow my interests and piqued my curiosity as I asked what was out there, seeking more ways of human-powered travel across the horizon. The ongoing personal developmental process of actively participating in multisport added new challenges to life's puzzle at every stage.

By using the knowledge gained from each previous multisport accomplishment, we inform what we can do now and what we can aim to do in the future.

FINAL NOTES

If you are not sure where to start after this, one idea is to start with a walk.

In 1963, President Kennedy challenged Americans to a 50-mile walk. My dad and others of his generation remember this and feel it is ingrained in their psyche as the endurance event to go for, if you ever go for any. The nation was ignited, and family walks were taken across our city and others around America. This was perhaps the modern rebirth of ultradistances for normal people. Attorney General Robert F. Kennedy decided to take the challenge, hiking 50 miles as well. The next day he went ice skating with his children.

I encourage you to go for a walk. See if there are any bodies of water along the way. Maybe try a dip. Maybe hop on a bike or scooter after or play on a playground like it is an obstacle course during. Go horseback riding on your next vacation. Try SUP or SUP yoga. Ice skate at an outside rink this winter. When your kids are invited to a party at the trampoline park, jump too. Try that lazy river running class or the wave pool aqua fitness one at your rec center. Find your version of multisport to be energized, alive, and engaged with the world around you. Multisport allows you to push your limits and live life to your max. Get unstuck.

Stay sharp. Multisport lets you start small, so start with a walk, end with a run, and try it all in between.

Go Multisport!

Multisport is a wild way to add fun to your life, challenge yourself in multiple ways inside and out, and explore your world. The possibilities and choices are numerous and expandable for wherever you are in your individual journey. Plan, plot, push, discover, innovate, and break ground with multisport. Multisport gives you tremendous opportunities to change your workout routine and habits by introducing new sports and new sport combinations. The benefits include longevity, cross training, self-sufficiency, a way to combat restrictions, and new sporting knowledge.

We have learned the who, what, why, how, when, and where behind the new multisport and how it places the emphasis on your own self-propelled experience. You can now build your own multisport events that last hours, days, or longer with human-powered sports, multiuse concepts, and a solid collection of defined sporting systems.

We also know that you can multisport anywhere using what you have around you and your own creativity. Seek inspiration from the multisport events and tenets included here to establish your own based on your interests and enthusiasm.

Multisport gives you a reason and a way to explore locally and globally over land, sea, air and beyond. It is an all-weather, all-season activity that fits your timeline. Multisport encourages trying something new and travels with you. Multisport links and connects the world outside your door and provides a way to involve others in your sporting lifestyle.

Add fun, challenge, and exploration to your world, and *Go Multisport!*

ABOUT THE AUTHOR

Jennifer Strong McConachie is a multisport endurance athlete competing in running, swimming, triathlons, adventure racing, and paddling. She trains for mountain ascents around the world, including several of the Seven Summits. An Outward Bound graduate, she is also a Fellow in the Royal Geographical Society and member of The Explorers Club. She has a degree in Journalism, Mass Communications and Public Relations as well as several certifications in fitness teaching including from the American Council on Exercise. Jennifer is also an award-winning marketing and PR executive for global brands and organizations. As a professional speaker, presenter and trainer, Jennifer leads groups and workshops on business goal setting and leadership. Her previously published works include *Go Far: How Endurance Sports Help You Win At Life,* which combines endurance racing and Jennifer's unique life philosophy to create winning strategies for life's many challenges.